COMIC CHARACTERS OF SHAKESPEARE

By John Palmer

POLITICAL CHARACTERS OF SHAKESPEARE

COMIC CHARACTERS OF SHAKESPEARE

JOHN PALMER

MACMILLAN AND CO., LIMITED
ST. MARTIN'S STREET, LONDON
1946

COPYRIGHT

PRINTED IN GREAT BRITAIN

CONTENTS

▼

PUBLISHERS' NOTE

The five studies contained in this volume, though complete in themselves, represent only part of the much longer work JOHN PALMER had planned. They were finished shortly before his death in 1944.

INTRODUCTION

'THIS world', said Horace Walpole, 'is a comedy to those who think, a tragedy to those who feel'. The aphorism is well-worn, having served as a text for many essays on the comic, as distinguished from the tragic, approach to men and things.[1]

It is a true saying, as far as it reaches, and false for anything, which means nearly everything, that lies beyond. Therein it smacks of the period. English thinkers in the eighteenth century, with a few splendid exceptions, were tidy in their habits, almost as tidy as their French contemporaries, from whom, in despite of King George, who gloried in the name of Briton, they took their fashions in dress, deportment, philosophy and letters. It assumes that characters in a comedy, if we are to laugh at them, must be presented with detachment and that characters in a tragedy, if we are to weep for them, must be presented with sympathy. We might otherwise find the comic characters uncomfortably pathetic or the tragic characters unseasonably ridiculous. It explains why the French for generations insisted on keeping their heads in a comedy and losing their hearts in a tragedy. It explains why so many comic writers have valiantly insisted that they were satirical, unfeeling rogues, inviting us to laugh contemptuously at silly or wicked people. It explains why so many tragic writers have piously refrained from allowing their common sense to blunt their uncommon sensibility. It inspires the Bergsonian assumption that laughter is a social gesture whose evolutionary purpose is to keep men sensitive to their environment and that it is the business of comedy to correct excess, whether in the fool or the philosopher:

> La parfaite raison fuit toute extrémité
> Et veut que l'on soit sage avec sobriété.

Comedy, according to Walpole, is an act of judgment. We are to

---

[1] Including an essay on Comedy by the present author published years ago, in which with the staggering insolence of youth he surveyed the whole field of human laughter from a cabinet minister chasing his hat in Palace Yard to Falstaff, between the sheets, babbling of green fields.

suppose that a comic character is a personage, presented for our deri-sion, in whom some folly of the time or vice of nature is anatomised. We are invited to behold the activities of mortal men as they must appear to a reasonable being sufficiently disinterested to find them persistently amusing. We are summoned in that mood, to laugh heartily or to smile complacently at absurdities and misfortunes which we know to our cost to be anything but a laughing matter for those whose interests, passions, foibles and weaknesses are engaged.

Note, however, that even the participants in a comedy or tragedy can themselves be aware of the antithesis. Persons involved in a comical situation often exclaim: 'If this were not so terribly funny it would be really tragic'. Persons involved in a tragical situation ex-claim just as often: 'If this were not so dreadfully serious it would be really funny'. In these two exclamations Walpole's distinction is partially justified. There *are* two sides, the comic and the tragic, to almost every predicament. But Walpole's clear-cut opposition here reaches its limit. For it presupposes that the heart is idle when the head is active, and that the head ceases to function when the heart is in control. It denies that a man may laugh and be sorry at the same time, relish the humour of his own distresses, deride the fool and yet acknowledge a companionship in his folly, smile at extravagances to which he is himself as liable as their victim, be diverted by the exhibition of a weakness and yet retain a lively sympathy for the weakling, delight in the misadventures of a rascal and yet recognise him for a kindred spirit. It ignores, in fact, the essential quality of humane comedy, which only appears when the distinction between heart and head is obliterated; for, in the finest and most satisfying laughter, there is just that element of emotional sympathy which Walpole declared to be incompatible. This element is present even in the laughter provoked by a satirist who, in deriding the things which he wishes to destroy, invites us to recognise that we are all equally liable to the errors, vanities and obsessions at which he aims. There is more fellow-feeling than detachment even in the comedies of Molière if we look below the surface and reflect upon the source and quality of our amusement, and when we come to the comedies of Shakespeare the distinction simply vanishes.

Shakespeare's detachment is admittedly absolute in the sense that he never appears in his own person. His characters, once created, exist in their own right. Shakespeare is silent when Titania speaks. But this is not the detachment of a man who thinks as opposed to the sympathy of a man who feels. It implies on the contrary the complete negation of such a man. Shakespeare's detachment was from himself and not from his creatures. Almost the whole secret of his power is the facility with which he identifies himself imaginatively with all sorts and conditions of men and women. He is almost incapable of the judicial approach. In the very act of holding up a villain to reprobation or a fool to derision he enters their minds and hearts. He is entirely *objective* in that the personality of William Shakespeare avoids the stage and that the personal equation is never allowed to distort the independence and veracity of his portraiture. He is entirely *subjective* in the sense that he completely identifies himself in imagination with the ideas and sentiments portrayed. He loses himself in the thing he contemplates; suppresses himself in the act of giving life to the creatures of his fancy. The secret of his genius lies in what Keats described as his 'negative capability'. He is never Shakespeare; he is in turn Hamlet, Cressida or Caliban.

Comedy, if it implies detachment of the author from his characters and their presentation for intellectual judgment undisturbed by emotion, was consequently foreign to his whole process of creation. Where the comic writer, within the narrow limits assumed by Walpole, stands aloof to survey mankind in the light of reason, Shakespeare, presenting a fool, is the fool incarnate; and, laughing at a fool, laughs at something which he requires us to recognise as flesh of our flesh and bone of our bone. Shakespeare, in fact, never wrote a comedy within the commonly accepted sense of the term or put on the stage a comic character for the critical diversion of an audience assumed to be celestially immune from the normal infirmities of human nature. Once or twice, during that strange period in his creative progress when his infinite charity of mind was in eclipse, he resolutely tried his hand at this kind of spectacle. The result was a play like 'Troilus and Cressida' or 'Measure for Measure', in which he deliberately struck the Olympian attitude, taking his stand for a moment with the wise gods who 'laugh at us while we strut to our confusion'. But how soon was the satirical mood abandoned! Shakespeare set out in derision, but nature was too strong for him. He begins in a mood of artificial detachment, but cannot sustain it. Almost at once he is caught up in the perplexities and distresses of his victims. Cressida, while he remembers to be a satirist, is presented as one of the 'daughters of the game', to be numbered among the 'sluttish spoils of opportunity'. Troilus is a poor fool who dotes upon a false mistress. But at the mere contemplation of these unhappy lovers, exchanging frail vows while Sir Pandarus holds the door, Shakespeare relents. Cressida is startled by the same lark, herald of the morn, that sang so out of tune in the ears of Juliet and she loses Troilus to as sad a strain as Shakespeare ever wrote:

> Injurious time now with a robber's haste
> Crams his rich thievery up, he knows not how:
> As many farewells as be stars in heaven,
> With distinct breath and consign'd kisses to them,
> He fumbles up into a loose adieu,
> And scants us with a single famish'd kiss,
> Distasted with the salt of broken tears.

Who, after that, can read 'Troilus and Cressida' in the mood of comic detachment? Even more startling is the collapse of Shakespeare, the comic censor, in 'Measure for Measure'. The play is colder and more deliberate in its cynicism than 'Troilus and Cressida', and there is less fellowship in this play than in any other of his writing. Its good providence is an 'old fantastical duke of dark corners' and its heroine a lady whose self-centred virtue chills us to the marrow. The rest form such a group as were never before or since assembled on the author's stage; among them one Claudio, who esteems his own life more highly than his sister's chastity. But beside Shakespeare the heartless comedian stood Shakespeare the poet, to whom no human heart was a stranger, and at the supreme moment, when the satirist was putting his finishing touch of obloquy upon his wretched victim, the poet suddenly took charge and the

man who has been exposed to our derision breaks into a cry that
makes him one with ourselves:

> Ay, but to die, and go we know not where;
> To lie in cold obstruction and to rot;
> This sensible warm motion to become
> A kneaded clod;
>
> To be imprison'd in the viewless winds,
> And blown with restless violence round about
> The pendent world;
>
>   'tis too horrible!
> The weariest and most loathèd worldly life
> That age, ache, penury and imprisonment
> Can lay on nature is a paradise
> To what we fear of death.

The sentiment is not heroic, but there can be no pretence that Shakespeare is here making that critical gesture of the spirit which is commonly expected of the comic dramatist.

If Shakespeare, at a time when, for some reason as yet unfathomed,
he was casting himself for the part of Thersites in a distracted world,
was unable to sustain the mood of comic detachment, it is not sur-
prising that in the comedies which reflect his more natural genius he
was quite incapable of bringing his fellow men to judgment. His
comic characters are not so much persons at whom we are invited to
laugh as persons who please us to the point of laughter only in so far
as we are able and ready to identify ourselves with their moods and
perceptions. Comedy which springs from the strain of cruelty which
many find to be inseparable from laughter, which excludes all sympathy with the victim, is to Shakespeare so uncongenial that, even
when he takes for his subject a stock figure of fun, he tends to
humanise it to such a degree that actors and critics are often tempted
to exaggerate the element of pathos in his achievement. Shylock, the
Jew, presented in the grotesque framework of a plot intended to
throw into relief the least engaging qualities of his race, becomes the
almost tragic representative of a persecuted minority. This comic
character turns suddenly upon his audience: *If you prick us, do we not*

bleed? That is a question which no comic character has any right to ask. There are moments when Shakespeare deals with Shylock as Molière dealt with Harpagon. Indeed, the scene in which the Jew alternately rejoices to hear of Antonio's misfortunes and rages to hear of Jessica and his lost ducats is the most Molièresque scene he ever wrote. But Shakespeare could not keep to this level. The Jew, even in this comic display of greed and passion for revenge, reflexively stimulated so that he may exhibit them at a maximum, grows too terrible for comedy: *I would my daughter were dead at my foot, and the jewels in her ear! Would she were hearsed at my foot, and the ducats in her coffin!* And he grows at the same time too human in his torment: *Hath not a Jew eyes? hath not a Jew hands, organs, dimensions, senses, affections, passions?*

Shakespeare's refusal to draw any clear distinction between a comic character, at whom a wholly reasonable person may laugh, and a tragic character, with whom a normally sensitive person must feel in sympathy, was not the deliberate decision of an artist consciously pursuing a method, but the natural expression of his imaginative reaction to human nature. For him the dichotomy did not exist. This explains the fact, so disconcerting to his French critics and to the pre-romantic commentators, that some of his most notable comic characters turn up at the most unexpected moments and in the most unlikely places. Juliet's nurse springs to life in a tragedy. Polonius treads in the footsteps of a ghost from the grave. The Alsatia in which Falstaff flourishes as a Lord of Misrule is just one province in a land where an English king dies of a broken heart and an English prince self-consciously prepares to assume his inheritance. The partitions are thin which divide comedy and tragedy in Shakespeare's world. Polonius in the tragedy of 'Hamlet' is more recognisably a comic character than Orsino in the comedy of 'Twelfth Night' or Jaques in the comedy of 'As You Like It'.

Who, then, *are* the comic characters and when are they truly comic? In what does the comic element consist?

No general or precise answer can be given to a question which ignores the essential quality of Shakespeare's imaginative process. All we can do is to take, as we find them, characters which all the world agrees to be amusing and to inquire into the source of our peculiar pleasure. We shall expect in advance to discover that the secret of Shakespeare's comedy lies in the quality of his imaginative reaction to life itself. We shall find ourselves watching, in an infinite variety of moods and forms, that constant interplay of thought and feeling, detachment and sympathy, ridicule and affection, serene judgment and passionate self-identification which lies at the heart of his genius.

There is a recurrent device in the comedies of Shakespeare which offers a preliminary clue to the labyrinth into which we are about to venture. When Malvolio reads a famous letter writ in the sweet Roman hand, and so falls into the pit of absurdity digged for him by his adversaries, the contrivers of his disgrace are behind a hedge in Olivia's garden watching his every gesture and heartlessly enjoying the performance. When Benedick and Beatrice are caught in the snare laid for them by Don Pedro and his friends, the architects of their discomfiture are there to take pleasure in the mischief. When the King of Navarre and his backsliding companions are exhibited as false to their academic vows, there is a progressive company of eaves-droppers, each of them prompt to enjoy the decline and fall of his recreant predecessor. When Titania is enamoured of an ass, there is Oberon to triumph in her delusion, and when a quartet of young lovers is plagued in A Wood near Athens, there is Puck to delight in their follies. Shakespeare, in making fun of his characters, usually contrives that there shall be someone present on the stage to hold a watching brief for the comic muse. The spectator thus perceives not only the victim but the unsympathetic witnesses by whom the victim is derided. He is invited to realise that there are two parties to the jest and to divide his sympathies. There are occasions, too, when even the contrivers of the mischief cease to be entirely merciless. Even Puck has his moments of sympathy:

> Cupid is a knavish lad
> Thus to make poor females mad.

Oberon frankly relents in the prosecution of his trick upon the fairy queen: *Her dotage now I do begin to pity;* and Sir Toby feels a twinge of compunction when the jest against Malvolio has been carried to extremes: *I would we were well rid of this knavery.*

Satirical comments by onlookers upon the stage provoke the onlookers in front to react in favour of the persons who are made ridiculous. The dramatist says in effect: 'Here, as in life, is someone who is made to look foolish and here, too, are people quick to flout them and proudly immune from their distresses; but you, who see the comedy as a whole, might just as easily find yourself on one side of the hedge as the other'.

Sympathy, then, and not satire, is the inspiration of Shakespeare's comedy. The appeal of his comic characters, even as we laugh at them, is to the touch of nature which makes the whole world kin. A delicate balance is constantly sustained in the persons of the play between the folly which makes them laughable and the simplicity which makes them lovable, between the frailties or faults which lay them open to rebuke and a common humanity with ourselves which calls for charity and secures for them an immediate understanding. The balance varies from scene to scene and from play to play. Each comedy shows the essential geniality of Shakespeare's comic approach in a different mood, and the mood is so nicely determined that each of the characters, to be seen without distortion, must appear in its own environment. Malvolio would be as out of place in the Forest of Arden as Bully Bottom in Olivia's garden or as Rosalind in A Wood near Athens. Each of these comic characters is but one figure in a composition where every touch has reference to the work as a whole; and to study any one of them apart from its context would be like looking at a single figure taken from a picture by Michael Angelo or Botticelli consigned as an illustration of 'detail' to an artist's portfolio. The melancholy Jaques is an effectively comic philosopher as the co-mate and brother-in-exile of the banished Duke. Orsino is an exquisitely comic man of sentiment as suitor to Olivia. Benedick is a vivaciously comic misogynist as the predestined husband of Beatrice. Remove them from a setting whose colour, form and rhythm—the very air they breathe—are all nicely calculated to delineate and illumine their absurdity and the spell is broken.

Shakespeare himself once made the mistake of removing one of his comic characters from his natural surroundings; and the victim of this experiment, though of all his creatures the most robust and self-sufficient, nearly died of his translation. Sir John Falstaff, at home in Eastcheap and on Shrewsbury Field, moving as freely in low life as in high policy, well nigh perished in the bourgeois confines of Windsor Park. His great figure could only be truly seen against the violent background of civil war, the full-blooded mischief of highway robbery and the swaggering humours of the tavern. There is nothing perceptibly wrong with Falstaff in his misadventures with the merry wives. There is no decline in his eloquence, no abatement of relish, no change even of the means whereby he is inspired to show his essential quality—for Falstaff is never more himself than when he rises irrepressibly above the ignominies designed for him by the lilliputians. Yet the critics find him at Windsor diminished to a shadow of his former self. They feel that something rather terrible has happened to Falstaff and they are right. He is living out of his time and place. He has become an awful example in a homily of good life. His environment forces us to acknowledge that he is not respectable. It is as though Tom Jones had strayed into a novel by Jane Austen.

Shakespeare committed this act of comic misprision in deference to a royal request that he should show Falstaff in love. He could not go quite so far as that and it was a miracle that he should have gone as far as he did without killing his man outright. Let us take this warning to heart and insist on viewing these comic characters of Shakespeare under the lights and shadows that play upon them in the gardens and palaces, the fields and taverns, the streets and chambers, where they meet and move for our pleasure.

I

BEROWNE

Love's Labour's Lost

THE greatest comic dramatist since Aristophanes—assuming that
Shakespeare is ineligible to compete—sprang into fame with a genial
satire upon the metaphysical exquisites of the blue *salon* of the
Marquise de Rambouillet. Molière, when he came to Paris in 1658,
impudently challenged the established arbiters of literary taste with
a comedy as devastating in its effect upon the fashionable wits and
poets of the day as the little child's remark upon the Emperor's new
clothes in Andersen's fairy tale. *Les Précieuses Ridicules,* by a young
dramatist who had recently arrived from the provinces, destroyed
in a gale of laughter a literary and social sect which no one until that
moment had ventured to find ridiculous.

By a happy coincidence Shakespeare, at an almost identical point
in his career, came upon the London stage with a 'Pleasant Conceited
Comedy Called Love's Labour's Lost', in which the exquisites of his
own time and country were brought to book. It is instructive to
compare the spirit in which these two men of genius approached a
very similar enterprise. Their subject was the same; they had a like
intention, which was to be amusing at the expense of the verbal and
sentimental affectations of the period; their audience in both cases
was a select company of persons passionately addicted to the follies
at which they were invited to laugh. These follies, moreover, had a
superficial resemblance.

Here, then, is a unique opportunity of observing two great
comedians at work upon the same theme, writing under much the
same conditions, basing their comic appeal on the same conflict of
broad humanity with social artifice, of common sense with intellectual extravagance, of truth to nature with the distortions of fancy.
Everything seems to be prompting them to the same conclusions
and consequences. The result is, nevertheless, a contrast at all points

A

between the two achievements and a revelation of essential qualities that divide their authors in everything but their firm grasp of the abiding realities of the human spirit.

The first point of contrast lies in the fact that Molière, in mocking the exquisites of the blue *salon*, was deriding a coterie whose standards of taste and whose approach to literature and life were quite definitely alien and pernicious. There could be no comedy in France such as Molière was determined to write, till the *alcovistes,* not born of a father and mother but secreted by the alcove as an oyster secretes the pearl, ceased to plot their way on the Map of the Tender Passion towards the City of Sensitive Esteem, through forty leagues of Friendly Sentiment, to the Hamlet of Gallant Addresses, where a mistress was expected tenderly to entertain her lover without enjoyment and substantially to enjoy her husband with aversion.[1] Molière was always much more than a satirist, but he was often provoked by his enemies into announcing that satire was what he intended and, in the preface to *Les Précieuses Ridicules,* he explicitly declared that 'the correction of social absurdity must at all times be the matter of true comedy'. In writing his first pugnacious comedy he deliberately challenged and destroyed something for which he felt an actively wholesome contempt. These exquisites were not only corrupters of taste and manners; they were veritable misleaders of youth, setting up false standards of sentiment and behaviour in whose presence common sense and good feeling were almost ashamed to show their honest faces. Molière, moved to a genuine derision, was determined to put out of court and countenance absurdities which were naturally antipathetic to his genius.

Very different was the mood and purpose of Shakespeare in his 'pleasant conceited comedy'. Admittedly he set out to make fun of the sophisticated and metaphysical wits of London. But he was ridiculing absurdities which, on occasion, he was quite happy to share with his contemporaries and he amused his audience with a display of virtuosity in an art of which he was himself a notable practitioner. There is nothing destructive or contemptuous in his

[1] For Molière's Battle with the Exquisites see Chapter VIII of the present author's *Molière.*

handling of these pedantical lords and subtle ladies. Their sentimental encounters, in which phrases and fancies run extravagantly wild for our pleasure, are mocked with an indulgence that implies affection rather than reprobation. Who, after all, was Shakespeare to castigate man or woman for exuberance in 'conceit', extravagance in the manipulation of words, profligacy in the pursuit of a fair image, prodigality in the expense of imagination? How could Shakespeare, who was one day to present on his stage Benedick and Beatrice, allow himself to suggest that Berowne and Rosaline were too silly for words? Admittedly he invites us to laugh at their antics. Berowne is often exquisitely ludicrous. But all this is chaff rather than satire, provoking us to laugh companionably at a fool with whom his author is ready to change shoes at any moment.

The difference of mood in which Molière and Shakespeare undertake their strange adventure—*l'étrange entreprise de faire rire les honnêtes gens*—strikingly reveals the temperamental abyss that lies between the French and the English comedian. It is also to be noted that, despite many striking similarities, there is a very real difference between the objects of their mirth. The French exquisites of the seventeenth century carried to excess a tradition which had lost its vitality. They had played with words till the words had lost their meaning. They had refined upon their sentiments till there was no real feeling left. 'These people', wrote La Bruyère, wise after the event, 'left to the commonalty the art of speaking intelligibly. One thing, expressed with no great clarity, led to another even more obscure, which was in turn improved upon by the delivery of riddling redes which were always greeted with prolonged applause. From an exaggeration of what they described as delicacy of feeling and refinement of expression, they finally reached the point of being entirely ambiguous and of failing to understand even one another'. The extravagant conceits of the Euphuists of Elizabethan England, though equally complicated, were not anaemic. They were rather the result of an abnormally high blood pressure. For the French exquisites words were like coins worn thin with too much jingling. For the Elizabethans every word came fresh from the die. They loved the glitter and music of their chime. Shakespeare, introducing

Armado in 'Love's Labour's Lost'—the figure of fun in whom the
English Euphuists were mocked—uses this very simile:

> A man in all the world's new fashion planted,
>   That hath a *mint* of phrases in his brain:
> One who the music of his own vain tongue
>   Doth ravish like enchanting harmony.

and Berowne, making ready to welcome the Euphuist, declares:

> Armado is a most illustrious wight,
> A man of fire-new words, fashion's own knight.

Armado, 'child of fancy', is brought into the play to 'relate in high-
born words', things which will certainly exceed the modesty of
nature; and we are invited to share the pleasure which the King of
Navarre means to take in his performances:

> How you delight, my lords, I know not I,
> But I protest I love to hear him lie,
> And I will use him for my minstrelsy.

This game, we perceive, is to be played with the bright counters
of a speech whose unexplored resources were as exciting a challenge
to the poets of Elizabethan England as were the shores of the Spanish
Main to her gentlemen adventurers.

The difference between Molière, setting out to correct social
absurdity, and Shakespeare, promising his audience rare sport
among the Euphuists, is incarnate in the principal person of the play.
Berowne is the first of a long line of characters in whom Shakespeare,
to the extent in which he mocks the victims of his comedy, renders
them only the more attractive.

Shakespeare will so easily lose the satirical purpose with which he
started, and so often provoke us to wonder whether he is ridiculing
excess in his characters or sharing their intoxication, that it is well to
get the main design of the play clearly cut in our minds before
allowing outsiders to be absorbed in its details. The King of Navarre
induces a group of noble lords to go with him into intellectual re-
treat. They will for the space of three years forswear the company of

women, eat only one meal a day, fast a day in every week and sleep
for not more than three hours in the night. They hope by this discipline to attain a knowledge of things 'hid and barred from common
sense' which is 'study's god-like recompense'. Unfortunately for
these prospective monks of the new learning the King of Navarre is
obliged to receive an embassy from the King of France which comes
to discuss matters of state. The embassy is led by an accomplished
and beautiful princess attended by her ladies. The King of Navarre
will not admit them into his house but he cannot refuse to parley
with them beyond the gates. So, in the words of the Victorian
Euphuist, Walter Pater, we have 'on one side, a fair palace: on the
other the tents of the Princess of France; . . . in the midst, a wide space
of smooth grass. The same personages are combined over and over
again into a series of gallant scenes'. The princes, of course, fall in
love with the ladies and each tries to conceal his treason:

> For oaths are straws, men's faiths are wafer-cakes
> And hold-fast is the only dog, my duck;—

as was to be said one day by that fiercest of all the Euphuists, Ancient
Pistol.

The princes woo the princesses in disguise, with intricate tributes
in verse and pyrotechnical displays of ingenious wit and pretty sentiment. Finally there is a general recantation. Artifice is abandoned
and nature carries the day.

Berowne has a very special place in this playful satirical design.
Along with the rest he is mocked by his author and is a target for the
ladies. But he fully appreciates the comedy of his predicament. He
speaks for nature, though caught in the toils of artifice; and, at the
end, delivers the moral of the piece in which he has, in effect, played
the part of Chorus on his author's behalf. It is as though Shakespeare
had said: 'Here, if you like, is a satire; but, if you insist on laughing
at these fantastical persons, please remember that we are all painted
with the same brush and note that, if this fellow Berowne, with
whom I am obviously on excellent terms, has my permission to
moralise the spectacle, that is only because he has been well content
to play the fool for your diversion'.

Let us now follow Berowne more closely through the peripatetics of his adventure.

The King of Navarre announces his plan:

> Therefore brave conquerors—for so you are,
> That war against your own affections
> And the huge army of the world's desires—
> Our late edict shall strongly stand in force,
> Navarre shall be the wonder of the world,
> Our court shall be a little academe,
> Still and contemplative in living art.

Berowne declares that he is ready to study with the King for three years but protests against the conditions:

> O, these are barren tasks, too hard to keep,
> Not to see ladies, study, fast, not sleep.

He would prefer swearing to a better purpose:

> Come on then—I will swear to study so,
> To know the thing I am forbid to know:
> As thus—to study where I well may dine[1]
>   When I to feast expressly am forbid,
>   Or study where to meet some mistress fine
>   When mistresses from common sense are hid.

He nevertheless signs the articles and is the first to perform a brilliant euphuistic exercise on the theme of the comedy, in which, while showing himself to be a master of the game, he stoutly maintains that it is a sport contrary to nature. There is little profit in poring upon books or naming the stars:

> Why, all delights are vain, but that most vain
> Which, with pain purchased, doth inherit pain—
> As painfully to pore upon a book,
>   To seek the light of truth, while truth the while

[1] Compare the declaration in which Molière's Sosie cuts the knot of his metaphysical perplexities:
> Le véritable Amphitryon
> Est l'Amphitryon où l'on dîne.

Doth falsely blind the eyesight of his look:
   Light, seeking light, doth light of light beguile:
So ere you find where light in darkness lies,
Your light grows dark by losing of your eyes.

Study is like the heaven's glorious sun,
   That will not be deep-searched with saucy looks:
Small have continual plodders ever won,
   Save base authority from others' books.
These earthly godfathers of heaven's lights,
   That give a name to every fixèd star,
Have no more profit of their shining nights,
   Than those that walk and wot not what they are. . . .
Too much to know, is to know nought but fame:
And every godfather can give a name.

Light, seeking light, doth light of light beguile. Dr. Johnson said:
'The whole sense of this jingling declamation is only this—that a
man by too close study may read himself blind, which might have
been told with less obscurity in fewer words'. He was evidently not
amused.[1] But the Euphuists who attended the play in 1597, 'as presented before Her Highness this last Christmas', found the words
neither too many nor obscure. Words, for Johnson and his contemporaries, had lost their magic. They were not things to play with,
but things to be rounded up and impounded in a dictionary. They
must be definite, precise and serviceable. For the Elizabethans, however, they might still be used as spells and incantations. The jingling
declamation in which Johnson found but a single meaning evoked
in Shakespeare's auditors a manifold delight. For them there were
overtones in the jingle. They saw Johnson's plain sense of the
matter, namely that a man may read himself blind. But they caught
also the suggestion that a man in seeking more knowledge may

---

[1] The whirligig of time brings in his revenges. Coleridge ridiculing the poetic
diction of Johnson himself was fond of quoting the following couplet from 'The
Vanity of Human Wishes':
      Let observation with extensive view
      Survey mankind from China to Peru;
which is as much as to say: Let observation with extensive observation observe
mankind extensively.

grow less in wisdom. They found in this line a light that sparkled and changed—light of the eyes, light in the printed word, light of the intelligence and a light beyond even that—a light divine that may be lost in following its earthly reflection.

Berowne goes into the adventure with no illusions as to the sequel:

> I'll lay my head to any goodman's hat,
> These oaths and laws will prove an idle scorn.

He is first of the noble lords to fall from grace and there is no more pleasant conceited speech in this pleasant conceited comedy than that in which he announces his predicament:

> And I—
> Forsooth in love, I that have been love's whip!
> A very beadle to a humorous sigh,
> A critic, nay, a night-watch constable,
> A domineering pedant o'er the boy,
> Than whom no mortal so magnificent—
> This whimpled, whining, purblind, wayward boy,
> This Signior Junior, giant-dwarf, Dan Cupid,
> Regent of love-rhymes, lord of folded arms,
> Th'anointed sovereign of sighs and groans,
> Liege of all loiterers and malcontents,
> Dread Prince of Plackets, King of Codpieces,
> Sole imperator and great general
> Of trotting paritors—O my little heart!
> And I to be a corporal of his field,
> And wear his colours like a tumbler's hoop.

So much for the general. What follows is more particular:

> Nay, to be perjured, which is worst of all;
> And among three to love the worst of all—
> A whitely wanton with a velvet brow,
> With two pitch-balls stuck in her face for eyes,
> Ay and, by heaven, one that will do the deed,
> Though Argus were her eunuch and her guard!
> And I to sigh for her, to watch for her,
> To pray for her, go to: it is a plague
> That Cupid will impose for my neglect
> Of his almighty dreadful little might. . . .

> Well, I will love, write, sigh, pray, sue, and groan—
> Some men must love my lady, and some Joan.

Longaville, Dumaine and the King wear their folly with a difference. They have not Berowne's capacity to appreciate their own absurdity. There is an exquisite gradation in their successive exposure. First comes Berowne inditing a sonnet, but before he can make an end, the King approaches and he too carries a script. Berowne climbs into a tree and overlooks his companions as one after another they reveal their discomfiture and hide in turn from the next arrival:

> Like a demigod here sit I in the sky,
> And wretched fools' secrets heedfully o'er-eye.

Securely aloft, he overhears how 'love may vary wit'. He observes how each offender pretends to innocence and denounces his predecessor, till at last he descends to chide all three:

> You found his mote; the king your mote did see;
> But I a beam do find in each of three. . . .
> O, what a scene of fool'ry have I seen,
> Of sighs, of groans, of sorrow, and of teen.

Finally he is himself unmasked and shares in the general disgrace.

Berowne, however, is the first of the irrepressibles who in the Elysian Fields acknowledge Falstaff for their leader. He snatches a victory for nature from the defeat of pretension:

> Sweet lords, sweet lovers, O let us embrace!
>   As true we are as flesh and blood can be—
> The sea will ebb and flow, heaven show his face;
>   Young blood doth not obey an old decree:
> We cannot cross the cause why we were born;
> Therefore of all hands must we be forsworn.

And now he is ready to break into his great speech in praise of fair women:

> From women's eyes this doctrine I derive—
> They are the ground, the books, the academes,
> From whence doth spring the true Promethean fire.

> A lover's eyes will gaze an eagle blind;
> A lover's ear will hear the lowest sound,
> When the suspicious head of theft is stopped;
> Love's feeling is more soft and sensible
> Than are the tender horns of cockled snails;
> Love's tongue proves dainty Bacchus gross in taste.
> For valour, is not Love a Hercules,
> Still climbing trees in the Hesperides?
> Subtle as Sphinx, as sweet and musical
> As bright Apollo's lute, strung with his hair;
> And, when Love speaks, the voice of all the gods
> Make heaven drowsy with the harmony;

and so he advances to his practical conclusion:

> Then fools you were these women to forswear;
> Or, keeping what is sworn, you will prove fools.
> For wisdom's sake, a word, that all men love;
> Or for love's sake, a word that loves all men;
> Or for men's sake, the authors of these women;
> Or women's sake, by whom we men are men;
> Let us once loose our oaths, to find ourselves,
> Or else we lose ourselves to keep our oaths.

The sport, however, is not yet concluded. These sophisticated gentlemen have so far acknowledged the laws of nature as to forswear their unnatural enterprise, but they have still to win the ladies, and they set about it, not in the downright way of simple courtship, but with strange pastimes—masked as Russians, with a conned speech for 'a holy parcel of the fairest dames', with music and the King's petition that his Princess will 'vouchsafe some motion to it', with a splitting of jests and metaphors in which they are pitifully mocked and routed:

> The tongues of mocking wenches are as keen
>   As is the razor's edge invisible,
> Cutting a smaller hair than may be seen:
>   Above the sense of sense.

The remainder of the comedy turns less upon a quartet of lovers irretrievably forsworn as on the conduct of the ladies they are pledged to overcome. Who, then, are these ladies and what is their part in the play?

The Princess of France has been unfairly neglected. Shakespeare has not yet at his command the gifts which he will shortly bestow on his comic heroines—the music of Viola, the voluble precision of Rosalind, the glitter of Beatrice, the eloquence of Portia. But the Princess of France already bears the stamp royal. She has just that commingling of good sense and lively imagination, of quick feeling and clear thinking, of instinctive reserve and an equally instinctive candour, which distinguishes all Shakespeare's happy women who give away their hearts without losing their heads. She is the first flower upon a branch that was to bear blossoms of a deeper colour and a headier scent, all different and yet so unmistakably from the same stem; and there is a freshness in this first budding of an im-mortal type which has its special charm. Her first sedate challenge to the King, not without a hint of mischief, confronts him neatly with his own preposterous dilemma:

> I hear your grace hath sworn out house-keeping:
> 'Tis deadly sin to keep that oath, my lord,
> And sin to break it.

Her comment on the recreant lovers flies straight to the target:

> None are so surely caught, when they are catched,
> As wit turned fool. Folly, in wisdom hatched,
> Hath wisdom's warrant, and the help of school,
> And wit's own grace to grace a learned fool;

and at the last, upon news of her father's death, she announces her departure with an exquisite grave courtesy:

> I thank you, gracious lords,
> For all your fair endeavours, and entreat,
> Out of a new-sad soul, that you vouchsafe
> In your rich wisdom to excuse, or hide,
> The liberal opposition of our spirits,
> If over-boldly we have borne ourselves
> In the converse of breath—your gentleness

Was guilty of it. Farewell, worthy lord:
A heavy heart bears not a nimble tongue.

She puts the King and his fellow suitors in their place firmly but with the same courtesy:

We have received your letters, full of love;
Your favours, the ambassadors of love;
And in our maiden council rated them
At courtship, pleasant jest, and courtesy,
As bombast and as lining to the time:
But more devout than this in our respects
Have we not been, and therefore met your loves
In their own fashion, like a merriment.

Her final verdict tempers justice with mercy. She is willing to surrender but only upon fair terms and proofs of honour:

KING: Now, at the latest minute of the hour,
Grant us your loves.

PRINCESS: A time methinks too short
To make a world-without-end bargain in:
No no, my lord, your grace is perjured much,
Full of dear guiltiness; and therefore this—
If for my love (as there is no such cause)
You will do aught, this shall you do for me:
Your oath I will not trust, but go with speed
To some forlorn and naked hermitage,
Remote from all the pleasures of the world;
There stay until the twelve celestial signs
Have brought about the annual reckoning.
If this austere insociable life
Change not your offer made in heat of blood,
If frosts and fasts, hard lodging and thin weeds,
Nip not the gaudy blossoms of your love,
But that it bear this trial, and last love:
Then, at the expiration of the year,
Come challenge me, challenge by these deserts,
And by this virgin palm now kissing thine,
I will be thine.

Shakespeare took more care to provide this early comedy with an appropriate and finished conclusion than he showed in some of his later works. The Princess of France maintains to the last the serenity and poise which contrast so effectively with the wayward and extravagant behaviour of her royal suitor. Zestfully offering 'There's no such sport as sport by sport o'erthrown', she never loses her hold upon reality in pursuit of its shadow. She is adorably serious. The King, embarking upon his fantastic adventure, grandly exclaims:

> Let fame, that all hunt after in their lives,
> Live registred upon our brazen tombs.

The Princess, when she chides herself for seeking to shed the poor deer's blood in order to show her skill, discards this last infirmity of noble minds:

> And, out of question, so it is sometimes:
> Glory grows guilty of detested crimes,
> When for fame's sake, for praise, an outward part,
> We bend to that the working of the heart.

Rosaline, the first of Shakespeare's dark ladies, is second only to the Princess of France in securing pride of place for the women of the play. She is whole-hearted in her affection and generous in her praise:

> Berowne, they call him—but a merrier man,
> Within the limit of becoming mirth,
> I never spent an hour's talk withal.
> His eye begets occasion for his wit,
> For every object that the one doth catch
> The other turns to a mirth-moving jest,
> Which his fair tongue—conceit's expositor—
> Delivers in such apt and gracious words,
> That aged ears play truant at his tales,
> And younger hearings are quite ravishèd,
> So sweet and voluble is his discourse.

But she is of the Shakespearean sisterhood who, though won, must still be wooed:

> How I would make him fawn, and beg, and seek,
> And wait the season, and observe the times,

> And spend his prodigal wits in bootless rhymes,
> And shape his service wholly to my hests,
> And make him proud to make me proud, that jests!

She plagues her lover with an inverted tenderness and in the knowledge that he is a man who prizes spirit in a woman and looks for no easy victory. He must do penance with the rest and prove his claim to be wise and faithful. Her sentence is well delivered:

> The world's large tongue
> Proclaims you for a man replete with mocks,
> Full of comparisons and wounding flouts;
> Which you on all estates will execute
> That lie within the mercy of your wit. . . .
> To weed this wormwood from your fructful brain,
> And therewithal to win me, if you please—
> Without the which I am not to be won—
> You shall this twelvemonth term from day to day
> Visit the speechless sick, and still converse
> With groaning wretches; and your task shall be,
> With all the fierce endeavour of your wit,
> To enforce the painèd impotent to smile;

and she concludes in wisdom:

> A jest's prosperity lies in the ear
> Of him that hears it, never in the tongue
> Of him that makes it.

Berowne defends himself as well as he may—and not so badly either. It may be true, as Rosaline affirms, that 'better wits have worn plain statute caps', but—

> your beauty, ladies,
> Hath much deformed us, fashioning our humours
> Even to the opposèd end of our intents.

Let these damsels therefore bear some part of the blame for what 'in us hath seemed ridiculous':

> As love is full of unbefitting strains,
> All wanton as a child, skipping and vain,

Formed by the eye, and therefore, like the eye
Full of strange shapes, of habits and of forms,
Varying in subjects as the eye doth roll
To every varied object in his glance.

Therefore, ladies,
Our love being yours, the error that love makes
Is likewise yours: we to ourselves prove false,
By being once false for ever to be true
To those that make us both—fair ladies, you.
And even that falsehood, in itself a sin,
Thus purifies itself and turns to grace.

But Berowne has the grace to know that he is beaten and the humour to appreciate his discomfiture:

Thus pour the stars down plagues for perjury.
    Can any face of brass hold longer out?
Here stand I, lady—dart thy skill at me,
    Bruise me with scorn, confound me with a flout,
Thrust thy sharp wit quite through my ignorance,
    Cut me to pieces with thy keen conceit.

His final repentance is devout and his promise of amendment made without reserve:

Taffeta phrases, silken terms precise,
    Three-piled hyperboles, spruce affectation,
Figures pedantical—these summer-flies
    Have blown me full of maggot ostentation.
I do forswear them, and I here protest,
    By this white glove (how white the hand, God knows!)
Henceforth my wooing mind shall be expressed
    In russet yeas and honest kersey noes.

Thus, in this pleasant conceited comedy, simple nature and good sense prevail over subtle sentiment and false conceit. All follies are redeemed and none is left in the stocks. In the conduct of plot and character the author keeps his wonted mean between sympathy and satire. It is yet more significant that in the Euphuistic embroideries of his theme Shakespeare shows the same tendency to identify himself

with the object of his derision. He means to mock these fine gentlemen for their preciosity, but, when he comes to write their verses,
we are often in doubt whether to admire their skill or smile at their
perversity. We begin to laugh and are caught by a melody. We
come to scoff and remain to pray that the music may continue.
Berowne, of whom it is said that every word is a jest and every jest
but a word, suddenly slips a line into his sonnet:

> Those thoughts to me were oaks, to thee like osiers bowed;

and we feel that Shakespeare, lost in the object of his mirth, has given
him something for which no poet need crave indulgence. The
King's sonnet, precious enough in all conscience, admirably sustains
the conceit on which it is founded and, though we may be jolted
into mockery as we ride along, it lands us at last in a crystal coach
upon the broad highway of the muses:

> So sweet a kiss the golden sun gives not
>   To those fresh morning drops upon the rose,
> As thy eye-beams, when their fresh rays have smote
>   The night of dew that on my cheek down flows:
> Nor shines the silver moon one half so bright
>   Through the transparent bosom of the deep,
> As doth thy face through tears of mine give light:
>   Thou shin'st in every tear that I do weep,
> No drop but as a coach doth carry thee:
>   So ridest thou triumphing in my woe.
> Do but behold the tears that swell in me,
>   And they thy glory through my grief will show:
> But do not love thyself—then thou wilt keep
> My tears for glasses, and still make me weep.

If this be parody it is such that only a poet, indulgently smiling at a
brother's extravagance, could write. It is written in sport, but might
have fallen from the sheaf inscribed to Mr. W. H. Shakespeare is
smiling at his own excess, standing aside as it were, from the solemn
achievement of his younger muse, presenting it for our merriment.
The pure comedian, flouting absurdity, would have written for his
poetasters effusions that were wholly ridiculous. Molière, satirising a

precious marquis, indites for him an impromptu whose pretentious inanity is heightened by the absurd comments of his admirers:

> Oh, oh, je n'y prenais pas garde:
> Tandis que, sans songer à mal, je vous regarde,
> Votre œil en tapinois me dérobe mon cœur.
> Au voleur, au voleur, au voleur, au voleur!

Congreve composes for Mr. Brisk after the same fashion:

> For as the sun shines every day,
> So, of our coachman I may say,
> He shows his drunken fiery face,
> Just as the sun does, more or less.
> And when at night his labour's done,
> Then too, like heaven's charioteer the sun,
> Into the dairy he descends,
> And there his whipping and his driving ends;
> There he's secure from danger and from bilk,
> His fare is paid him, and he sits in milk.

There is no fellow-feeling in Molière for Mascarille or in Congreve for Mr. Brisk, as they spout and posture to their coteries of half-wits. The mood, intention and result are entirely different. Shakespeare can laugh at his Euphuists and love them, too.

Nor does Shakespeare's sympathy so generously extended to the finer wits of his comedy stop short at grosser manifestations of the literary fashion at which he aims. His wits 'have been at a great feast of languages and stolen the scraps' and upon such as 'have lived long on the alms-basket of words' he can be downright satirical:

> This fellow pecks up wit, as pigeons pease,
> And utters it again when God doth please.

> A' can carve too, and lisp: why, this is he
> That kissed his hand away in courtesy.
> This is the ape of form, monsieur the nice,
> That when he plays at tables chides the dice
> In honourable terms; nay, he can sing
> A mean most meanly, and, in ushering,
> Mend him who can. The ladies call him sweet.
> The stairs as he treads on them kiss his feet.

B

But how he delights in Holofernes, the schoolmaster, speaking by the book; Sir Nathaniel, the priest, adoring a text; Don Armado, the fantastical knight, composing a letter; Costard, the clown, who must needs be in the fashion, too! What zest he imparts to the display of their talents! They have all drunk of the cup of Dionysus, and Shakespeare, sharing their intoxication, comprehends their contempt for any dullard to whom the Pierian spring supplies no headier draught than plain mineral water:

> Sir, he hath never fed of the dainties that are
>   bred in a book.
> He hath not eat paper, as it were; he hath not
>   drunk ink:
> His intellect is not replenished, he is only an
>   animal, only sensible in the duller parts:

Holofernes blesses God for his gift and Shakespeare enjoys it with him even as he parodies its exercise:

This is a gift that I have, simple, simple; a foolish extravagant spirit, full of forms, figures, shapes, objects, ideas, apprehensions, motions, revolutions. These are begot in the ventricle of memory, nourished in the womb of pia mater, and delivered upon the mellowing of occasion. . . . But the gift is good in those in whom it is acute, and I am thankful for it.

These fantastical fellows have their own standard of excellence and Shakespeare enjoys their company. Listen to Sir Nathaniel, the curate, and Holofernes, the schoolmaster, discussing the qualities of good conversation and the merits of Don Armado:

SIR NATHANIEL: I praise God for you, sir. Your reasons at dinner have been sharp and sententious; pleasant without scurrility, witty without affection, audacious without impudency, learned without opinion, and strange without heresy. . . I did converse this quondam day with a companion of the king's, who is entitled, nominated, or called Don Adriano de Armado.

HOLOFERNES: Novi hominem tanquam te. His humour is lofty, his discourse peremptory: his tongue filed, his eye ambitious, his gait majestical, and his general behaviour vain, ridiculous, and thrasonical. . . . He is too picked, too spruce, too affected, too odd as it were, too peregrinate as I may call it.

SIR NATHANIEL: A most singular and choice epithet. (*Draws out his table-book.*)

HOLOFERNES: He draweth out the thread of his verbosity finer than the staple of his argument. I abhor such fanatical phantasimes, such insociable and point-devise companions, such rackers of orthography.

Holofernes is undeniably a figure of fun, but Shakespeare identifies himself with his folly as completely as with the more delicate absurdity of Berowne, and in his boundless geniality suffers the pedant to rebuke with simple dignity the fine gentlemen who bait him when he brings on the Nine Worthies for their entertainment: *This is not generous, not gentle, not humble.*

Don Armado is admittedly a caricature, but he is no empty husk. To him also Shakespeare gives of his best and our mockery stands abashed when suddenly he, too, is touched with his author's magic and pleads for Hector: 'The sweet war-man is dead and rotten; sweet chucks, beat not the bones of the buried.'[1] Nor is he easily put down. Flouted by the lords and 'infamonized among potentates' he retains our respect even in confessing that he has no shirt and he retires with dignity:

For mine own part, I breathe free breath: I have seen the day of wrong through the little hole of discretion, and I will right myself like a soldier.

In his courtship of Jaquenetta he calls to mind, for all his absurdity, the wooing of Audrey by the melancholy wise man who was shortly to epitomise the seven ages of man and shows himself the more likeable fellow of the two. For Armado is in love—so deep in love that he is struck as speechless in the presence of his monosyllabic mistress as he is voluble in her absence:

ARMADA: Maid.
JAQUENETTA: Man.
ARMADO: I will visit thee at the lodge.
JAQUENETTA: That's hereby.

[1] Shakespeare, in the flush of his young genius, could not foresee that he would one day commit the very impiety which Don Armado here denounces. There is an odd thrill in these lines for those who have seen their author astray and beating the bones of the buried in 'Troilus and Cressida'.

>   ARMADO: I know where it is situate.
>   JAQUENETTA: Lord, how wise you are!
>   ARMADO: I will tell thee wonders.
>   JAQUENETTA: With that face?
>   ARMADO: I love thee.
>   JAQUENETTA: So I heard you say.
>   ARMADO: And so farewell.
>   JAQUENETTA: Fair weather after you!

And his devotion is put to a proof that brings him quite literally to earth:

> I am a votary; I have vowed to Jaquenetta
> To hold the plough for her sweet love three year.

Even in a ludicrous misemployment of words and fancies Shakespeare is seldom remote from his own felicity. 'Arts-man', says Armado, taking Holofernes by the elbow, 'perambulate. We will be singled from the barbarians'. He continues: 'It is the King's most sweet pleasure and affection to congratulate the princess at her pavilion in the posteriors of this day, which the rude multitude call the afternoon'. Holofernes snaps at this preposterous image: 'The posterior of the day, most generous Sir, is liable, congruent and measurable for the afternoon: the word is well called, chose—sweet and apt'. Mere foolery but nearly twenty years later Shakespeare's Menenius was to describe himself as more conversible 'with the buttock of the night than the forehead of the morning'. Or take the scene in which the King's gentlemen cap one another in finding similitudes for the peaked face of Holofernes—the head of a bodkin . . . a death's face in a ring . . . the face of an old Roman coin . . . the carved-bone face on a flask . . . the pummel of Caesar's falchion. It is a catalogue that beckons us forward to a certain tavern in Eastcheap where Sir John Falstaff will grow breathless with base comparisons: you starveling, you elf-skin, you dried neat's tongue . . . you tailor's yard, you sheath, you bow-case, you vile standing tuck!' Then, too, we come upon Armado and Moth seated beneath the trees in the Park of Navarre. 'Warble, child, make passionate my sense of hearing', prays Armado. 'Come, warble, come,' urges the melancholy Jaques in the Forest of Arden. The mood is consonate and the place contiguous.

Costard, the clown, is allowed a touch of nature which brings him to life and endears him to the spectator:

> COSTARD: 'I Pompey am, Pompey surnamed the Big'—
> DUMAINE: The Great.
> COSTARD: It is 'great,' sir.—'Pompey surnamed the Great,
> That oft in field with targe and shield did make my foe to sweat,
> And travelling along this coast I here am come by chance,
> And lay my arms before the legs of this sweet lass of France.'
> (*Casts down shield and sword.*)
> If your ladyship would say, 'Thanks Pompey,' I had done.
> PRINCESS: Great thanks, Great Pompey.
> COSTARD: 'Tis not so much worth; but I hope I was perfect. I made a little fault in 'Great'.

And Sir Nathaniel, the curate, driven from the scene by the mockery of the fine gentlemen who have not their author's embracing love for a simpleton, is accorded a testimonial which puts him, too, among those who are forever redeemed by the love of their creator:

> COSTARD: There, an't shall please you, a foolish mild man—an honest man, look you, and soon dashed. He is a marvellous good neighbour, faith, and a very good bowler: but for Alisander, alas you see how 'tis—a little o'erparted.

Molière, satirising a literary fashion in his *Les Précieuses Ridicules*, presented a group of exquisites which were not only true to the period but true of all the exquisites who ever lived. His characters were from life and there was not a phrase or gesture in his comedy which could not be matched from the conversation and behaviour of his originals. So long as complicated fashion is liable to corrupt natural simplicity his play will remain amusing and intelligible. He successfully avoided, in fact, the faults which he was denouncing, refraining from a preciosity which might have tempted him to multiply his local and personal allusions and would in time have rendered much of his comedy incomprehensible to posterity. Shakespeare's 'Love's Labour's Lost', though in essentials it is broader in humanity than Molière's play, has, on the contrary, become in places difficult and here and there forever meaningless even to the scholar. The reason, again, is to be sought in the fact that Shakespeare, less intent than Molière on the 'correction of social absurdity', is absorbed into the game from which Molière held aloof in a more critical frame of mind. Molière looked on at the follies which he denounced. Shakespeare romps whole-heartedly with his fools. His play is more in the nature of a family diversion in which intimate private jests are exchanged for the fun of the thing. To many of these witticisms we have lost the clue. They remain embedded in his play, to use the vivid metaphor of Dr. Dover Wilson, as 'persistent flies in its amber'. There is 'a crowd of ephemeral references and allusions which, undissolved, irritate as specks of grit irritate the eye'. Dr. Johnson, discussing these blemishes, charged the author with sacrificing permanent interest to personal satire. Shakespeare, he argues, in presenting Holofernes, was so bent on ridiculing the local schoolmaster that his portrait has little value for those who are unacquainted with the original. 'It is of the nature of personal invectives', Johnson writes, 'to be soon unintelligible: and the author that gratifies private malice, *animam in vulnere ponit*, destroys the future efficacy of his own writings and sacrifices the esteem of succeeding time to the laughter of a day.' Very trenchant and very true; but wholly irrelevant. There is no private malice in the presentation of Holofernes or Moth or Armado. There is not even a sustained criticism of their extravagance. If Shakespeare in this comedy sacrificed the esteem of succeeding time to the laughter of a day, it was not owing to any malice, private or general, but to a warm interest in his characters, and boundless pleasure in their oddities of mind.

It is possible by study and the exercise of imagination to recover something of that laughter of a day which for the casual reader is irretrievably lost.[1] But we are seeking here confirmation that in the

---

[1] Dr. Dover Wilson has recovered all but ninety per cent. of it. 'Love's Labour's Lost' has an irresistible charm and attraction for the best critics. Pater devotes to it one of his finest 'Appreciations'; Granville Barker one of his notable 'Prefaces' and

topicalities of the play as in its general design Shakespeare, so far from gratifying any private malice, was presenting a picture of contemporary manners to an audience which was more than ready to take everything in good part—that he was offering it, in fact, not a personal invective but, in the words of the title-page, a pleasant conceited comedy. Whether, in point of fact—as seems not at all unlikely—we may identify Holofernes with John Florio, Moth with Thomas Nashe, the little Academe of the King of Navarre with the group of Copernicans and black magicians whose poet was George Chapman, there can be no doubt whatever that 'Love's Labour's Lost', as played before the Queen in 1597, was a topical piece packed with open and covert allusions to a piece of social history in which many members of the distinguished audience had, in fact, themselves participated. His theme, moreover, was not only topical but dangerous. Shakespeare in the comic vein contrived in 'Love's Labour's Lost' to do precisely what he did more seriously, and just as successfully, in 'Richard II' and 'King John', namely to write a play bristling with perilous implications and to escape either censure or calumny because he wrote it with an entire absence of prejudice, putting a natural emphasis upon its broadly human as opposed to its narrowly social, political or sectarian aspects, exhibiting a tolerance that embraced every man in his humour, passions, affections, foibles and infirmities.[1] It was an almost unique achievement. His contemporaries seldom meddled with subjects of public or social interest without paying the penalty. Jonson, Nashe, Kyd, Chapman—all experienced the untender mercies of Star Chamber. To write a topical play under Elizabeth or James was to ask for trouble and in most cases to get it promptly and in full measure. But Shakespeare was never molested. He wandered freely in a world in which neither the Queen who was quite prepared to hang a man for witnessing a play with treason in it, nor the King who put Jonson in prison

Dr. Dover Wilson, in collaboration with Quiller-Couch, an 'Introduction' which is as sensitive to its enduring magic as it is erudite and ingenious in the elucidation of its fugitive allusions.

[1] See the present author's *Political Characters of Shakespeare*, published in 1945.

for a play which made fun of the Scots, ever challenged his conduct or authority.

To those who are unfamiliar with the social background to 'Love's Labour's Lost' it must seem impossible that it should contain anything perilous to life or liberty. The play is, nevertheless, charged with brimstone:

> Black is the badge of hell,
> The hue of dungeons and the School of Night.

The King of Navarre is here treading on dangerous ground and Berowne with his enigmatic praise of black ladies and commendation of ebony as a wood divine is inviting disaster. In the spring of 1593 the Queen's Privy Council were taking a sinister interest in a small society which counted among its initiates Chapman, Kyd and Marlowe, among the dramatists, and no less a person than Sir Walter Raleigh among the nobility. These men studied the stars; they were proficient in the art of numbers and were even suspected of raising the devil. A warrant was issued for Marlowe's arrest, but he was killed in a brawl before he could be brought to trial. Kyd was put to the torture. Raleigh, already in disgrace, was later examined by a special commission appointed to investigate his 'heresies'. Into the thick of all this comes Shakespeare, smiling, with a pleasant conceited comedy in his hand; and the comedy is presented to the Queen at Christmas. In it he presents a little academe of seclusive gentlemen who also study the stars and swear to sleep for only three hours in twenty-four. The play abounds in cryptic allusions to numbers and chapmen's tongues. Berowne sings the praises of sable beauty. But Shakespeare seems not to be in the least aware of his peril. He makes fun of these fantastical gentlemen, but it is all done in pure kindness of heart. His references to certain poets, head-over-heels implicated in some very dangerous proceedings, are not in the least censorious. He seems to be neither of one side nor the other. He promises a satire on the wicked and a castigation of fools; but the wicked prove on acquaintance to be excellent company and the fools are merely diverting. Was there ever a more striking example of charity in genius covering a multitude of sins any one of which was a hanging matter in the eyes of authority?

And so we revert to Berowne himself, who of all the characters in this strangely enchanting medley of wit and poetry most fully expresses its mood and purpose. For Shakespeare in Berowne is smiling not merely at follies with which after the fashion of his comic genius he puts himself for the time being in imaginative sympathy, but at folly to which he was himself as a poet peculiarly liable in his own person. There is in all that Berowne utters what Pater has described as 'a delicate raillery by Shakespeare himself at his own chosen manner . . . He has at times some of its extravagance or caricature also, but the shades of expression by which he passes from this to the "golden cadence" of Shakespeare's own most characteristic verse, are so fine that it is sometimes difficult to trace them . . . . That gloss of dainty language is a second nature with him: even at its best he is not without a certain artifice: the trick of playing on words never deserts him; and Shakespeare, in whose own genius there is an element of this very quality, shows us in this graceful, and, as it seems, studied, portrait, his enjoyment of it'.

Pater was concerned more with the literary than with the dramatic significance of Berowne. He sees in Berowne 'a reflex of Shakespeare himself, when he has just become able to stand aside from and estimate the first period of his poetry'. He is fascinated by that 'foppery' of language which 'satisfies a real instinct in our minds—the fancy so many of us have for an exquisite and curious skill in the use of words'. This, however, is but one aspect of the matter. Berowne is the first of Shakespeare's characters in which the essential quality of his comic genius becomes apparent. He is the first fine product of that imaginative process whereby Shakespeare identifies himself with the object of his mirth, thus combining in a single gesture of the spirit, detachment with sympathy, serene judgment with congenial understanding, the objectivity of a creating mind with an entire subjection of the imagination to the thing created.

To conclude all, the cuckoo sings:

> When daisies pied, and violets blue,
>   And lady-smocks all silver-white:
> And cuckoo-buds of yellow hue,
>   Do paint the meadows with delight:

> The cuckoo then, on every tree,
> Mocks married men; for thus sings he,
> > Cuckoo. . . .
> Cuckoo, cuckoo: O word of fear,
> Unpleasing to a married ear.
>
> When shepherds pipe on oaten straws,
> > And merry larks are ploughmen's clocks:
> When turtles tread and rooks and daws,
> > And maidens bleach their summer smocks:
> The cuckoo then, on every tree,
> Mocks married men; for thus sings he,
> > Cuckoo. . . .
> Cuckoo, cuckoo: O word of fear,
> Unpleasing to a married ear.

And the owl sings, too:

> When icicles hang by the wall,
> > And Dick the shepherd blows his nail:
> And Tom bears logs into the hall,
> > And milk comes frozen home in pail:
> When blood is nipped, and ways be foul,
> Then nightly sings the staring owl,
> > To-whit to-who. . . .
> A merry note,
> While greasy Joan doth keel the pot.
>
> When all aloud the wind doth blow,
> > And coughing drowns the parson's saw:
> And birds sit brooding in the snow,
> > And Marian's nose looks red and raw:
> When roasted crabs hiss in the bowl,
> Then nightly sings the staring owl,
> > To-whit to-who. . . .
> A merry note,
> While greasy Joan doth keel the pot.

Shakespeare withdraws from his little academe and destroys by example all that he has seemed to encourage by precept in his pleasant conceited comedy. The exquisites whom he was too kind to destroy as Molière destroyed those of a later day, fade away like bright figures in a tapestry as suddenly a window is thrown open upon a meadow in Warwickshire and in place of a gay and pretty masque of quaint lords and sweet ladies, Dick the shepherd blows his nail and greasy Joan doth keel the pot.

The author's script, enigmatic to the last, concludes with a sentence attributed to none of the characters: *The words of Mercury are harsh after the songs of Apollo.* Is there here a hint of the secret we are after? One would like to imagine that this Delphic line, printed large in the quarto, was a comment written on Shakespeare's MS by a friendly critic who had been struck by that peculiar quality of indulgence which distinguishes the comedies of Shakespeare from all others of his time.

These are the songs of Apollo, after which all other words come harsh upon the ear.

II

TOUCHSTONE

As You Like It

AMONG the dramatic styles enumerated by Polonius in announcing the players at Elsinore was the pastoral-comical. It was coming well into fashion at the beginning of the seventeenth century and Shakespeare was bound sooner or later to handle it. Pastoral-comical is not of course confined to the theatre. It satisfies the craving of civilised people in all ages to assume a simplicity which is, in effect, only a further step in sophistication. My lady of fashion fancies herself as a Dresden shepherdess; the raffish young gentleman sees himself piping on an oaten straw. Poets, painters and composers, great and small, have ministered down the ages to this affectation, which has been responsible for more bad verse, insipid pictures and commonplace music than has sprung from any other reputable source on Parnassus.

Shakespeare, writing his first draft of 'As You Like It' in 1593, could hardly forbear to remember that in Christopher Marlowe England had just lost an author who had made a very notable contribution to the sylvan muse:

> Dead shepherd, now I find thy saw of might,
> Who ever loved that loved not at first sight?

Spenser had published 'The Shepherd's Calendar' and Sidney his 'Arcadia'. Plays, poems and novels, in which the deceitful amenities of court and city life were contrasted with the simple pleasures of the countryside, were in high demand. The fashion had come from Italy and it had come to stay. There was as yet no Hazlitt to deplore its anaemic graces. Hazlitt described 'Arcadia', which in 1590 had started upon a triumphant career which was to carry it far and wide over Europe, as 'one of the greatest monuments of the abuse of intellectual power'. But by that time the pastoral-comical had flourished for over two centuries. Fletcher had sentimentalised it in

'The Faithful Shepherdess'; Ben Jonson had weighted it with his learning; in numerous masques Molière had collaborated with Corneille to give it liveliness and gravity; Inigo Jones had devised suitable costumes and appropriate settings for its nymphs, shepherds and divinities; Milton had converted it from pastoral-comical to pastoral-ethical in his 'Comus'; English cavaliers and French exquisites had flattered or flouted their mistresses in rustical odes, sonnets and impromptus; Marie Antoinette had postured as a dairymaid at Trianon, and Rousseau had written a political treatise in which it was assumed that man might solve all his social problems by making a fresh start from the state of nature.

Pastoral-comical, returning to the age of innocence, harks back to the mythology of the antique world. Its devotees are as conscientiously erudite as they are resolutely simple-minded. The shepherd courts his mistress in an eclogue and is passionate by the book. The nymph, in her daydreaming, quotes Ovid or, taking up her lute, extemporises a madrigal:

> Love in my bosom like a bee
> doth suck his sweet:
> Now with his wings he plays with me,
> now with his feet.
> Within mine eyes he makes his nest,
> His bed amidst my tender breast,
> My kisses are his daily feast;
> And yet he robs me of my rest. . . .

and keeps it up for as many stanzas as you please.

All the divinities in the Graeco-Roman calendar must be invoked to picture her:

The blush that gloried Luna when she kist the shepherd on the hills of Latmos was not tainted with such a pleasant dye as the vermilion flourisht on the silver hue of [her] countenance; her eyes were like those lamps that make the wealthy covert of the heavens more gorgeous, sparkling favour and disdain; courteous and yet coy, as if in them Venus had placed all her amorets, and Diana all her chastity. The trammels of her hair, folded in a caul of gold, so surpassed the burnisht glister of the metal as the sun doth the meanest star in brightness: the tresses that fold in the brows of Apollo were not half so rich to the sight; for in her hairs it seemed love had laid herself in ambush, to entrap the proudest eye that durst gaze upon their excellence.

The sylvan scene is set with an artifice that matches a wooing of swains who, if their mistresses cannot be moved in the mother tongue, are ever ready to try the effect of a Latin tag or a French sonnet:

The ground where they sat was diapred with Flora's riches, as if she meant to wrap Tellus in the glory of her vestments: round about in the form of an amphitheatre were most curiously planted pine trees, interseamed with lemons and citrons, which with the thickness of their boughs so shadowed the place that Phoebus could not pry into the secret of that arbour; so united were the tops with so thick a closure that Venus might there in her jollity have dallied unseen with her dearest paramour. Fast by, to make the place more gorgeous, was there a Fount so crystalline and clear that it seemed Diana with her Dryads and Hemadryads had that spring as the secret of all their bathings.

The pleasures of a simple life are recommended with an artful duplicity:

Envy stirs not us, we covet not to climb, our desires mount not above our degrees nor our thoughts above our fortunes. Care cannot harbour in our cottages, nor do our homely couches know broken slumbers; as we exceed not in diet, so we have enough to satisfy; and, Mistress, I have so much Latin, *Satis est quod sufficit.*

Their love-gifts are apples and chestnuts and it would stain the honour of a shepherdess to set the end of passion upon pelf. But they are well read in the satyrical Roman rogue: *quarenda pecunia primum, post nummos virtus.* Crowns have crosses when mirth is in cottages; but your shepherd, though he be dying for love, is not inaccessible to argument and knows that a maid who is beautiful, virtuous *and wealthy* has three deep persuasions to make love frolic. The nymph, though she shroud her pains in the cinders of modesty, protects her face from the sun with a chaplet of roses and is not unaware of the fetching picture she makes in a petticoat of scarlet covered with a green mantle. They would hoodwink you into believing that, taking bag and bottle to the field, where they have such cates as country state may allow, sauced with sweet content and engaging prattle, they have learned to forswear courtly junkets; but we begin to have some doubt about the sincerity of this rustic conversion when we find the lady taking good care to provide herself with a kirtle so fine that she seems some heavenly nymph harboured in country attire or when the gentleman comes in apparelled all in tawny to signify that he is forsaken, on his head a garland of willow and on his sheephook two sonnets as labels of his loves and fortunes.

The learnèd reader will by now have realised that he is in the forest of Arden—not yet Shakespeare's Arden but the Arden of Thomas Lodge, whose 'Golden Legacie', attributed to Euphues and fetched from the Canaries, was brought to London in 1590 and published with a dedication to the Lord Chamberlain of her Majesty's household.

Lodge's tale of Rosalynde is a pretty piece of work, perhaps the most instructively typical of its kind in the English language. It is worth reading for itself and it has an interest for the historian who seeks acquaintance with the social and literary taste of the period. For those who have tried so often and so unsuccessfully to come upon Shakespeare in the act of diverting to his purpose a unique and original source its value is inestimable. No older play has been found to stand between the author of 'As You Like It' and the original fount of his inspiration. Shakespeare's comedy comes straight out of the novella of Thomas Lodge—theme, characters and incidents. The cribbing is everywhere manifest. Yet though everything is taken, nothing remains the same. The likenesses everywhere serve only to display the difference. In no play of Shakespeare are his native wood-notes more freshly heard. There is dew on every shoot. In no play is the language so apt, lucid and free. The dramatist finds his material sophisticated, mannered, artfully ingenuous, studied in playfulness, affected in sentiment. This he transmutes into something which conveys an impression of unfettered simplicity. Light and shade in this comedy ripple to the movement of forest leaves in the wind. It is as voluble as a bird in April, as happy as a summer day is long. Here, as the mood takes them, men fleet the time carelessly as in the golden world or under the shade of melancholy boughs lose and neglect the creeping hours of time. Shakespeare, imparting a genuine innocence to a style that merely affects it, plays the same trick with the characters and incidents. The wicked brother in Lodge's tale, the usurping Duke, the loves of Rosader (Orlando) and Rosalynde, the reformation of Saladyne (Oliver) and his wooing of Aliena (Celia) are treated with all the solemnity and particularity that befits a pastoral tale of knights and ladies. Shakespeare changes none of the incidents; some of the smallest details crop up unexpectedly in a phrase or turn of the action. But as with the style, so with the matter. The transmutation is complete. The quarrel between the brothers, which in Lodge is a desperate sustained feud, full of sound and fury, is presented in Shakespeare's comedy as a boyish squabble, to be taken just as seriously as the plot requires and no more:

OLIVER: Know you where you are, sir?

ORLANDO: O, sir, very well: here in your orchard.

OLIVER: Know you before whom, sir?

ORLANDO: Ay, better than him I am before knows me; I know you are my eldest brother, and in the gentle condition of blood you should so know me: the courtesy of nations allows you my better, in that you are the first-born, but the same tradition takes not away my blood, were there twenty brothers betwixt us: I have as much of my father in me as you, albeit I confess your coming before me is nearer to his reverence.

OLIVER: What, boy!

ORLANDO: Come, come, elder brother, you are too young in this.

OLIVER: Wilt thou lay hands on me, villain?

ORLANDO: I am no villain: I am the youngest son of Sir Rowland de Boys, he was my father, and he is thrice a villain that says such a father begot villains.

Lodge expends as much time on the bad brother's conversion as on the adventures of Rosalynde. Shakespeare takes the bad brother for his plot but never takes him seriously as a person and throws him into Celia's arms at the end of the story with a nonchalance which, among other odd consequences, entails the presence of a lioness in the heart of Warwickshire. Lodge winds up his romantic pastoral with a battle in which the banished duke lays on 'such loade upon his enemies that he showed how highly he did estimate of a crown'. The usurper is slain and the reader invited to reflect that 'such as neglect their father's precepts incur much prejudice'. Shakespeare winds up his comedy with a graceful litany that pleasantly mocks its own formality:

PHEBE: Good shepherd, tell this youth what 'tis to love.
SILVIUS: It is to be all made of sighs and tears,
　　　　And so am I for Phebe.
PHEBE: And I for Ganymede.
ORLANDO: And I for Rosalind.
ROSALIND: And I for no woman.

SILVIUS: It is to be all made of fantasy,
　　　　All made of passion, and all made of wishes,
　　　　All adoration, duty and observance,
　　　　All humbleness, all patience, and impatience,
　　　　All purity, all trial, all observance;
　　　　And so am I for Phebe.
PHEBE: And so am I for Ganymede.
ORLANDO: And so am I for Rosalind.
ROSALIND: And so am I for no woman.

But Shakespeare's 'translation' of the 'Golden Legacie' into his own sweet style is only half the miracle. For he uses here his old trick—the trick played in 'Love's Labour's Lost'—of throwing himself heart and soul into a convention and at the same time of subjecting it to the searching eye of the comic muse.[1] How dulcetly lovelorn is his quartet of amorists! Shakespeare plays the game to perfection. But, suddenly: 'Pray you, no more of this,' exclaims Rosalind, ''tis like the howling of Irish wolves against the moon.' It is a final fling of mother nature against pastoral-comical in which the author merrily libels his own performance. Shakespeare creates his illusion of a golden world, imposing on our imagination with an imperious felicity; but, once we are securely naturalised within its borders, we become aware that beside us, forever whispering, is an ironic spirit which, knowing what it loves, can smile indulgently on what it knows. Shakespeare leads us into the forest of Arden in all good

[1] See above, p. 25.

c

faith. This is a place where civilised men seek release from themselves in a return to nature. How delightful! Yet, at the same time,
how preposterous! For human nature in the forest of Arden is still
human nature—the same there as anywhere else and no-one can
escape it.

Shakespeare makes not the slightest effort to rusticate us among
the shepherds with set descriptions of fields, fountains, arbours and
glades or return us to an antique world with constant allusions to the
classical mythos. We are not impelled to be conscientiously agrestic.
We just slip away, as with a countryman returning home, to meet a
fool i' the forest, to find Orlando under a tree like a dropped acorn
or the melancholy Jaques lying beside the brook that brawls along
this wood. It is a forest that grows easily about us, and truant songs,
tuned to the sweet bird's throat, make us free of simple faring in all
its seasons:

> And this our life, exempt from public haunt,
> Finds tongues in trees, books in the running brooks,
> Sermons in stones and good in everything.

The winter wind bites and blows to the tune of 'Hey-ho the holly'; a
lover and his lass pass over the green cornfields in springtime. It is all
done so happily that Shakespeare, himself in a holiday mood, is
tempted to applaud his own felicity:

> Happy is your grace
> That can translate the stubbornness of fortune
> Into so quiet and so sweet a style.

The spell is immediate for those who are content to accept from
Shakespeare no more than the freedom of this sylvan city, who go
with Rosalind and Celia to liberty and not to banishment, who venture forth with Orlando and old Adam to light upon some settled
low content, who make one of the charmed circle who listen while
the sententious, melancholy Jaques moralises the spectacle of a
weeping deer or descants upon the seven ages of man. In the words
of 'Q', he who knows this Arden 'has looked into the heart of England and heard the birds sing in the green midmost of a moated
island'. But other and finer pleasures are in store. Shakespeare,

entering into Arden, yields his fancy to its enchantment, but does not therefore leave behind him his mother wit or sense of proportion. He takes with him as large a charter as the wind to blow on whom he pleases. His genial irony plays about each character in turn, his fellowship with these happy outlaws being all the more complete for his ability to see them in the light of nature. There is no desire or intention to bring them to judgment. Each abounds in his own grace or folly, his absolute quality emerging from his encounters and relationships with all the rest.

In most of Shakespeare's comedies there is a character who stands, as it were, at the centre. To get a clear view of the composition as a whole we must take up our position as near as possible beside him.

In 'Love's Labour's Lost' we found our point of reference for the comic values of the play in Berowne. In 'A Midsummer Night's Dream' it may be said concerning Bottom that 'if he come not, the play is marred'. For 'As You Like It' the author has named his own Touchstone. It is as though Shakespeare, setting out for Arden, where so many excellent poets have lost themselves in affected sentiment, mislaid their common sense in refining upon their sensibility and, in their self-conscious pursuit of nature, found themselves grasping a pale misfeatured shadow, had determined in advance to take with him a guide who should keep him in the path of sanity. Touchstone puts all things and every person in the play, including himself, to the comic test. Entering Arden with Touchstone you cannot go astray or mistake the wood for the trees.

It is his function to 'speak wisely what wise men do foolishly' and he loses no time about it. We are to accept him at once as no respecter of false persons:

TOUCHSTONE: Mistress, you must come away to your father.
CELIA: Were you made the messenger?
TOUCHSTONE: No, by mine honour, but I was bid to come for you.
ROSALIND: Where learned you that oath, fool?
TOUCHSTONE: Of a certain knight, that swore by his honour they were good pancakes, and swore by his honour the mustard was naught: now I'll stand to it, the pancakes were naught and the mustard was good, and yet was not the knight forsworn.

CELIA: How prove you that, in the great heap of your knowledge?
ROSALIND: Ay, marry, now unmuzzle your wisdom.
TOUCHSTONE: Stand you both forth now: stroke your chins, and swear by your beards that I am a knave.
CELIA: By our beards (if we had them) thou art.
TOUCHSTONE: By my knavery (if I had it) then I were: but if you swear by that that is not, you are not forsworn:

We are next to observe that this Touchstone has a lively sense of the fitness of things. Le Beau enters to tell the ladies of much good sport —how Charles, the wrestler, has broken the ribs of three proper young men, of excellent growth and presence:

TOUCHSTONE: But what is the sport, monsieur, that the ladies have lost?
LE BEAU: Why, this that I speak of.
TOUCHSTONE: Thus men may grow wiser every day. It is the first time that ever I heard breaking of ribs was sport for ladies.

We are to esteem him also as a loyal servant who, without any illusions as to the sequel, is ready at a word to 'go along o'er the wide world' with his mistress. This is no merely incidental touch. That Touchstone should set out in sturdy devotion, with an agreeably romantic expectation, is a fact essential to our appreciation of his quality. *His* part in the comedy is to shed the light of reality and common sense upon its fanciful figures and diversions. To play such a part he must be either a true cynic or one that affects his cynicism to mask a fundamentally genial spirit. Now a true cynic would be out of place in the forest of Arden. So Touchstone must be a thoroughly good fellow at heart. His brain may be as dry as the remainder biscuit after a voyage but he must be essentially a genial spirit. His acidity must be no more than skin-deep. He will see things as they are but without malice. He will have a keen flair for absurdity in people and things—not least for his own infirmities. He will, moreover, bring all things to the test of action, and the climax of *his* comedy will be to marry a slut so that he may embrace in reality the simple life which for his companions is no more than a holiday affectation.

How characteristic is his entry into the pastoral pleasaunce:

ROSALIND: O Jupiter! How weary are my spirits!
TOUCHSTONE: I care not for my spirits, if my legs were not weary.

ROSALIND: Well, this is the forest of Arden.
TOUCHSTONE: Ay, now am I in Arden, the more fool I. When I was at
home, I was in a better place, but travellers must be content.

This is wholesome correction and it comes most aptly between a
touching scene in which Adam displays 'the constant service of the
antique world', and our first encounter with Silvius and Corin—a
young man and an old in solemn talk. Note, too, how he pricks the
bladder of sentiment, not by rejecting its appeal, but by claiming a
share in its manifestations. The love of Silvius for Phebe and of
Rosalind for Orlando prompts him to declare: 'We that are true
lovers run into strange capers; but as all is mortal in nature, so is all
nature in love mortal in folly'; and he is driven to remember—nor
do we doubt the fidelity of the reminiscence—his own love for Jane
Smile and the kissing of her batler and the cow's dugs that her pretty
chopt hands had milked. All Touchstone is in that little speech—his
quaint pretension to philosophy and a capacity for romance, rooted
in nature but aware of its own excess. Jane Smile's hands were pretty
but the eye of the realist could not avoid noticing that they were chopt.

Touchstone, coming to terms with the simple life, cannot forget
that he has been, and remains, a courtier. He cannot refrain from
airing his graces and indulging his gentility. But there is no conceit
nor any hint of unkindness in his teasing of a country bumpkin. It is a
fault in him to show off in this way and he knows it for one:

It is meat and drink to me to see a clown. By my troth, we that have
good wits have much to answer for; we shall be flouting; we cannot hold.

But even his flouting has about it a quality which distinguishes him
from all the rest. Touchstone, 'above all things', is *interested* in people
and places and ways of life. He must get to the bottom of a subject
and take its measure. Of Corin he asks, as much in an honest desire
to know as in a spirit of mockery: 'Hast any philosophy in thee,
shepherd?' And when Corin expounds—

No more, but that I know the more one sickens, the worse at ease he is;
and that he that wants money, means and content is without three good

friends; that the property of rain is to wet and fire to burn; that good pasture makes fat sheep; and that a great cause of the night is lack of the sun—

Touchstone's rejoinder ('Such a one is a natural philosopher') is a shrewd companionable comment and no sneer. He must, as he confesses, be flouting. He takes an impish pleasure in maintaining that Corin, never having been at court or seen good manners, is damned; but Corin takes it all—as Touchstone intends it—in good part and serenely states his simple faith in the knowledge that, though it may be amiably mocked, it will nevertheless be respected:

Sir, I am a true labourer. I earn that I eat, get that I wear, owe no man hate, envy no man's happiness, glad of other men's good, content with my harm; and the greatest of my pride is to see my ewes graze and my lambs suck.

The whole thing is an epitome of Shakespeare's management of the pastoral theme. He presents the simple life with a most convincing innocence, but Touchstone is there to relate it justly to the scheme of things entire:

CORIN: And how like you this shepherd's life, Master Touchstone?
TOUCHSTONE: Truly, shepherd, in respect of itself, it is a good life; but in respect that it is a shepherd's life, it is naught. In respect that it is solitary, I like it very well; but in respect that it is private, it is a very vile life. Now in respect it is in the fields, it pleaseth me well; but in respect it is not in the court, it is tedious. As it is a spare life, look you, it fits my humour well; but as there is no more plenty in it, it goes much against my stomach.

Even the incomparable Rosalind, whose tide of wit and flush of love set her above any need of correction by the comic spirit, must be brought to the test if only to show how triumphantly she survives it. Orlando's rhymes are redeemed by the sincerity of his passion. But some of them have more feet than the verses will bear and the feet are lame. Indeed they are very tedious homilies of love, and all this she merrily declares. And Touchstone must also have his say. It is he who, on his author's behalf, must intimate very clearly that poetasters of the pastoral school are more deserving of mockery than imitation:

ROSALIND: 'From the east to western Ind,
            No jewel is like Rosalind.
            Her worth being mounted on the wind,
            Through all the world bears Rosalind.
            All the pictures fairest lined
            Are but black to Rosalind.
            Let no face be kept in mind
            But the fair of Rosalind.'

TOUCHSTONE: I'll rhyme you so eight years together, dinners, and suppers, and sleeping-hours excepted: it is the right butter-women's rank to market.

ROSALIND: Out, fool!

TOUCHSTONE: For a taste. . . .
            If a hart do lack a hind,
            Let him seek out Rosalind:
            If the cat will after kind,
            So be sure will Rosalind:
            Wintered garments must be lined,
            So must slender Rosalind.
            They that reap must sheaf and bind,
            Then to cart with Rosalind.
            Sweetest nut hath sourest rind,
            Such a nut is Rosalind.
            He that sweetest rose will find,
            Must find love's prick and Rosalind.

This is the very false gallop of verses. Why do you infect yourself with them?

ROSALIND: Peace, you dull fool! I found them on a tree.

TOUCHSTONE: Truly, the tree yields bad fruit.

Orlando's poem is itself a parody. Touchstone's is a parody twice over. Again he plays for us the author's trick. The pastoral exercise is pleasant in itself but still more pleasant for being so easily mocked.

Touchstone's place in the comedy is ridiculed as much by what he may do as by what his author carefully disallows. It is true that he makes antic hay of Orlando's verses and is reminded of Jane Smile on seeing his mistress in love, but he is not permitted to intrude into the courtship of Rosalind and Orlando. Rosalind stands in no need of correction save by her own true heart and wholesome intelligence.

She is her own touchstone and carries her own comedy in person. There is never any danger of our losing this child of nature in affectation or masquerade. Her first thought on hearing of Orlando in the forest is 'Alas the day, what shall I do with my doublet and hose?' Every word declares the impatient vivacity of a woman alive from head to heel. She must have an answer in one word to nine impetuous questions:

What did he when thou saw'st him? What said he? How looked he? Wherein went he? What makes he here? Did he ask for me? Where remains he? How parted he with thee? and when shalt thou see him again?

She cannot let Celia tell her tale but must interrupt her at every word:

ROSALIND: But doth he know that I am in this forest and in man's apparel? Looks he as freshly as he did the day he wrestled?

CELIA: It is as easy to count atomies as to resolve the propositions of a lover: but take a taste of my finding him, and relish it with good observance. I found him under a tree, like a dropped acorn.

ROSALIND: It may well be called Jove's tree, when it drops forth such fruit.

CELIA: Give me audience, good madam.

ROSALIND: Proceed.

CELIA: There lay he, stretched along, like a wounded knight.

ROSALIND: Though it be pity to see such a sight, it well becomes the ground.

CELIA: Cry 'holla' to thy tongue, I prithee; it curvets unseasonably. He was furnished like a hunter.

ROSALIND: O ominous! he comes to kill my heart.

CELIA: I would sing my song without a burthen—thou bring'st me out of tune.

ROSALIND: Do you not know I am a woman? when I think, I must speak. Sweet, say on.

Apparelled like a man and using her disguise to be securely wooed in proxy, she has no doublet and hose in her disposition and, caught by her own counterfeiting, swoons at the sight of a bloody napkin. Each new touch that reveals her is comedy distilled and carries its own commentary. So possessed is Rosalind by the comic spirit that, though she cannot endure her lover to be absent for two hours, she must recurrently mock at love with her mind as she yields to it unreservedly with her heart:

ROSALIND: Love is merely a madness, and I tell you deserves as well a dark house and a whip as madmen do: and the reason why they are not so punished and cured is, that the lunacy is so ordinary that the whippers are in love too.

ROSALIND: Am I not your Rosalind?
ORLANDO: I take some joy to say you are, because I would be talking of her.
ROSALIND: Well, in her person, I say I will not have you.
ORLANDO: Then in mine own person, I die.
ROSALIND: No, faith, die by attorney: the poor world is almost six thousand years old, and in all this time there was not any man died in his own person, videlicet, in a love-cause: Troilus had his brains dashed out with a Grecian club, yet he did what he could to die before, and he is one of the patterns of love: Leander, he would have lived many a fair year, though Hero had turned nun, if it had not been for a hot midsummer night; for, good youth, he went but forth to wash him in the Hellespont and being taken with the cramp was drowned, and the foolish chroniclers of that age found it was 'Hero of Sestos'. But these are all lies. Men have died from time to time, and worms have eaten them, but not for love.

No need here for Touchstone to keep the comedy sane and true; he would be out of place and could only spoil its perfection.

This applies also to the Duke with his co-mates and brothers in exile. Touchstone has expressed his own view of Arden and its amenities: when I was at home, I was in a better place. But Shakespeare, having translated the stubbornness of fortune into so quiet and so sweet a style, is not going to spoil the effect with flouting. The Duke, so far as he is corrected, corrects himself. We are never really deceived by his pastoral affectation, because he never wholly yields to it himself. It is always quite obvious that, for all his praise of life in the wilderness, he is making the best of a bad business. Old custom hath made this life more sweet than that of painted pomp; but adversity is a toad, even though it may wear a precious jewel in his head. This Duke, we realise, would normally prefer to find his

books in the library than to look for them in the running brooks, and
go to a well-appointed chapel for his sermons than to seek them in
stones. He is quick to remember the benefits of civilisation:

> ORLANDO: I thought that all things had been savage here,
>   And therefore put I on the countenance
>   Of stern commandment. But whate'er you are
>   That in this desert inaccessible,
>   Under the shade of melancholy boughs,
>   Lose and neglect the creeping hours of time;
>   If ever you have looked on better days;
>   If ever been where bells have knolled to church;
>   If ever sat at any good man's feast;
>   If ever from your eyelids wiped a tear,
>   And know what 'tis to pity and be pitied,
>   Let gentleness my strong enforcement be:
>   In the which hope I blush, and hide my sword.
> DUKE: True is it that we have seen better days,
>   And have with holy bell been knolled to church,
>   And sat at good men's feasts, and wiped our eyes
>   Of drops that sacred pity hath engendred:
>   And therefore sit you down in gentleness,
>   And take upon command what help we have
>   That to your wanting may be ministred.

A minute later he lets the cat out of the bag with a vengeance—

>   Thou seest we are not all alone unhappy:
>   This wide and universal theatre
>   Presents more woeful pageants than the scene
>   Wherein we play in.—

and at the last he embraces his return to the comforts of city life with
a most ingenuous alacrity:

>   First, in this forest, let us do those ends
>   That here were well begun and well begot:
>   And after, every of this happy number,
>   That have endured shrewd days and nights with us,
>   Shall share the good of our returnèd fortune,
>   According to the measure of their states.

The mellifluous Duke himself thus artlessly reveals the true quality of his rustication. Shakespeare accordingly refrains from contriving a meeting between him and Touchstone till the play is drawing to an end and even then the encounter is managed with considerable tact. Touchstone, in fact, simply ignores the happy exile and treats him instantly as a person of quality, adopting at once his courtliest manner and falling naturally back into his profession as a jester whose business it is to exercise his wit on behalf of the company:

TOUCHSTONE: Salutation and greeting to you all!

JAQUES: Good my lord, bid him welcome: this is the motley-minded gentleman that I have so often met in the forest: he hath been a courtier, he swears.

TOUCHSTONE: If any man doubt that, let him put me to my purgation. I have trod a measure—I have flattered a lady—I have been politic with my friend, smooth with mine enemy—I have undone three tailors—I have had four quarrels, and like to have fought one.

JAQUES: And how was that ta'en up?

TOUCHSTONE: Faith, we met, and found the quarrel was upon the seventh cause.

JAQUES: How seventh cause? Good my lord, like this fellow.

DUKE: I like him very well.　　. .

TOUCHSTONE: God 'ild you, sir, I desire you of the like; I press in here, sir, amongst the rest of the country copulatives, to swear and to forswear, according as marriage binds and blood breaks. . . . A poor virgin, sir, an ill-favoured thing, sir, but mine own—a poor humour of mine, sir, to take that that no man else will: rich honesty dwells like a miser, sir, in a poor house, as your pearl in your foul oyster.

DUKE: By my faith, he is very swift and sententious.

Whereupon he breaks into his brilliant analysis of the seven causes of quarrel between gentlemen, a virtuoso performance which concludes with the most celebrated of his quiddities: 'Your If is the only peace-maker: much virtue in If.'

The supreme test for Touchstone is his encounter with Jaques. But it is well, before we examine an incident which will determine our outlook on the entire comedy, to become more intimately acquainted with the man himself. Shakespeare affords us an opportunity in the episode of Touchstone's courting of Audrey. Here we behold the man who has no illusions concerning nature frankly responding to her call. The others merely trifle with her; Touchstone sees, hears and obeys:

> As the ox hath his bow, sir, the horse his curb, and the falcon her bells, so man hath his desires; and as pigeons bill, so wedlock would be nibbling.

He has found rich honesty, dwelling like a miser in a poor house, 'as your pearl in your foul oyster', and, having found it, has the courage of his convictions and will not let it go. His wooing of Audrey is at the same time a burlesque and a true reflection in nature of the three romantic courtships among which it intrudes. There is conscious irony in his claim to be pressing in 'among the rest of the country copulatives, to swear and to forswear, according as marriage binds and blood breaks', for none knows better than Touchstone himself that he alone is paying a genuine tribute to the ancient gods of the forest. His surrender to the great god, Pan, is the more complete, and certainly the more entirely comic, for his being clearly aware of what he is doing. He is still the courtier and he must still be flouting—even at the 'poor virgin, sir, an ill-favoured thing, sir, but mine own'. He will go so far as to suggest that 'not being well-married, it will be a good excuse hereafter to leave my wife'. But all these floutings are superficial. Touchstone's comedy, in fact, shows all the rest of the comedy in reverse. His wooing of Audrey is irony in action. Orlando, Rosalind, Silvius, Phebe and the rest affect their pastoral simplicity but remain entirely civilised. Touchstone affects his urbanity but is at heart a truly natural philosopher. None knows better than he what he is doing, for it is of the essence of his character to see himself as he sees everyone else in the play in detachment:

> A man may, if he were of a fearful heart, stagger in this attempt; for here we have no temple but the wood, no assembly but horn-beasts. But what though? Courage!

He begins his courtship with a double pun and a sidelong mockery of the whole pastoral outfit:

> I am here with thee and thy goats, as the most capricious poet, honest Ovid, was among the Goths—

but his deeds in plain English speak louder than the word-play in Latin.

Now that we begin to know our Touchstone we can have no doubt of what really happened upon his first encounter with Jaques. It is Jaques himself who describes the meeting:

> A fool, a fool! I met a fool i' th' forest,
> A motley fool—a miserable world!—
> As I do live by food, I met a fool,
> Who laid him down and basked him in the sun,
> And railed on Lady Fortune in good terms,
> In good set terms, and yet a motley fool.
> 'Good morrow, fool,' quoth I: 'No, sir,' quoth he,
> 'Call me not fool till heaven hath sent me fortune.'
> And then he drew a dial from his poke,
> And looking on it with lack-lustre eye,
> Says very wisely, 'It is ten o'clock:
> Thus we may see', quoth he, 'how the world wags:
> 'Tis but an hour ago since it was nine,
> And after one hour more 'twill be eleven,
> And so from hour to hour, we ripe, and ripe,
> And then from hour to hour, we rot, and rot—
> And thereby hangs a tale.' . . . When I did hear
> The motley fool thus moral on the time,
> My lungs began to crow like chanticleer,
> That fools should be so deep-contemplative;
> And I did laugh, sans intermission,
> An hour by his dial. . . . O noble fool!
> O worthy fool! Motley's the only wear.

Jaques relates how he has been amusing himself with a fool, but Touchstone, we perceive, has been amusing himself—and more to the purpose—with a philosopher. While Jaques was laughing at the fool, the fool was taking his measure and pulling his leg. Here Touchstone saw at once was a fashionable cynic, venting a shallow disappointment with men and things in well-turned homilies upon the way of the world. Playing up to his man the fool rails on Lady Fortune in good set terms. The philosopher is hooked and the fool lands his fish with a solemn descant upon the passage of time. Jaques, completely taken in, marvels that a fool should be so *deep-contemplative*.

We would give a good deal to have been present at this meeting, but Shakespeare decided otherwise and for a very good reason. If we had actually *seen* Jaques so obviously mocked, crowing like chanticleer but missing the whole point of the jest, we could never for a moment have regarded him as anything else but a figure of fun. But by merely *reporting* the incident Shakespeare leaves us to draw our own conclusions. He is not unwilling that Jaques should up to a point impose on his audience and be for the purposes of the play accepted at his own valuation. This melancholy gentleman was a popular stage character and none knew better than Shakespeare that a dash of sentimental cynicism goes down very well in a light comedy. Jaques is to be its purveyor and he must not therefore be too plainly exposed as a counterfeit philosopher who does not even know when the laugh is against him. Again our dramatist means to have it both ways. He will entertain us on the lower level with Jaques as a moralist and let those who like him thus be taken in if they will. But those who look a little deeper shall also have their fun.

Shakespeare so artfully plays this double game that it is quite possible to enjoy the comedy without allowing ourselves to become aware that the melancholy Jaques is, first to last, a purely comic character. Some critics have even gone so far as to compare him with Hamlet and most actors deliver his speech on the seven ages of man to a hushed audience as though it were a deep epitome of human experience. Shakespeare in fact has his little joke with the audience. Let those with a taste for Sir Oracle enjoy him as such. Observe how skilfully the dramatist builds him up. Our first reputed glimpse of him charms equally the eye and ear:

> FIRST LORD: Today my Lord of Amiens and myself
> Did steal behind him as he lay along
> Under an oak, whose antique root peeps out
> Upon the brook that brawls along this wood,
> To the which place a poor sequestred stag,
> That from the hunter's aim had ta'en a hurt,

Did come to languish; and, indeed, my lord,
The wretched animal heaved forth such groans,
That their discharge did stretch his leathern coat
Almost to bursting, and the big round tears
Coursed one another down his innocent nose
In piteous chase: and thus the hairy fool,
Much markèd of the melancholy Jaques,
Stood on th' extremest verge of the swift brook,
Augmenting it with tears.

DUKE: But what said Jaques?
Did he not moralize this spectacle?

FIRST LORD: O, yes, into a thousand similes.
First, for his weeping in the needless stream;
'Poor deer,' quoth he, 'thou mak'st a testament
As worldlings do, giving thy sum of more
To that which had too much': then, being there alone,
Left and abandoned of his velvet friends;
''Tis right,' quoth he, 'thus misery doth part
The flux of company': anon a careless herd,
Full of the pasture, jumps along by him
And never stays to greet him; 'Ay,' quoth Jaques,
'Sweep on, you fat and greasy citizens!
'Tis just the fashion; wherefore do you look
Upon that poor and broken bankrupt there?'

Note, however, that the spell is laid by First Lord and not by the subject of his tale. Not a word which Jaques is reported as saying shows real feeling or felicity. Antique root, sequestered stag, innocent nose, hairy foot, velvet friends, careless herd—it is an entrancing picture and Jaques gets credit for being included, though all he actually contributes is the moralising. His first actual appearance in the play is managed with equal cunning. There it is Amiens, singing of winter and rough weather, who lays the spell. Jaques again has all the advantage of being attractively presented. But his first words reveal him to the alert spectator as a misanthropist for whom all occasions are but opportunities to display an affected misanthropy. What is music to him?—*I can suck melancholy out of a song as a weasel sucks eggs.*

The craft with which Shakespeare builds him up is only equalled by the pertinacity with which he puts him down. Jaques comes off badly in his encounters with every person in the play. He is never happy unless he is showing off his melancholy to good advantage and he trails after each character in turn rather like a bore determined at all costs to corner his victim. Professing to love solitude, nothing but sheer rudeness can stay his eloquence or drive him away:

JAQUES: Will you sit down with me? and we two will rail against our mistress the world, and all our misery.

ORLANDO: I will chide no breather in the world but myself, against whom I know most faults.

JAQUES: The worst fault you have is to be in love.

ORLANDO: 'Tis a fault I will not change for your best virtue. I am weary of you.

JAQUES: By my troth, I was seeking for a fool when I found you.

ORLANDO: He is drowned in the brook—look but in, and you shall see him.

JAQUES: There I shall see mine own figure.

ORLANDO: Which I take to be either a fool or a cipher.

JAQUES: I'll tarry no longer with you. Farewell, good Signior Love.

ORLANDO: I am glad of your departure: adieu, good Monsieur Melancholy.

JAQUES: I prithee, pretty youth, let me be better acquainted with thee.

ROSALIND: They say you are a melancholy fellow.

JAQUES: I am so: I do love it better than laughing.

ROSALIND: Those that are in extremity of either are abominable fellows, and betray themselves to every modern censure worse than drunkards.

JAQUES: Why, 'tis good to be sad and say nothing.

ROSALIND: Why, then, 'tis good to be a post.

Note the sly comedy of that deliciously inappropriate observation—'Why, 'tis good to be sad *and say nothing*.' Jaques is the most loquacious person in the comedy. Rather than say nothing he will address a herd of deer and in the encounter with Rosalind he justifies his melancholy in a veritable spate of words:

I have neither the scholar's melancholy, which is emulation; nor the musician's, which is fantastical; nor the courtier's, which is proud;

nor the soldier's, which is ambitious; nor the lawyer's, which is politic; nor the lady's, which is nice; nor the lover's, which is all these: but it is a melancholy of mine own, compounded of many simples, extracted from many objects, and indeed the sundry contemplation of my travels, in which my often rumination wraps me in a most humorous sadness.

But Rosalind is not impressed:

And your experience makes you sad: I had rather a fool to make me merry than experience to make me sad—

and she dismisses him in a broadside which comes as near to downright chiding as it is her nature to come:

Farewell, Monsieur Traveller: look you lisp and wear strange suits; disable all the benefits of your own country; be out of love with your nativity, and almost chide God for making you that countenance you are; or I will scarce think you have swam in a gondola.

The unkindest cut of all comes, however, strangely enough, from the Duke. The Duke is the only person in the play who expresses a liking for Jaques. 'He hath been all this day to look for you,' says Amiens. 'And I', says Jaques, 'have been all this day to avoid him'. The Duke evidently enjoys a good argument. 'I love to cope him in these sullen fits, for then he's full of matter', declares his Grace. Jaques—and this is another sly stroke of comedy at his expense—is less fond of the Duke's company. Why? Because the Duke, if you please, *talks too much*. 'He is too disputable for my company', says Jaques. 'I think of as many matters as he, but I give heaven thanks and make no boast of them.' There is no-one like your much talker to resent loquacity in another.

Yet it is the Duke who, without any real provocation, suddenly rounds on his crony and pulls him to tatters:

JAQUES: Invest me in my motley; give me leave
To speak my mind, and I will through and through
Cleanse the foul body of th'infected world,
If they will patiently receive my medicine.
DUKE: Fie on thee! I can tell what thou wouldst do.
JAQUES: What, for a counter, would I do but good?

D

DUKE: Most mischievous foul sin, in chiding sin:
For thou thyself hast been a libertine,
As sensual as the brutish sting itself,
And all th'embossèd sores and headed evils,
That thou with licence of free foot hast caught,
Wouldst thou disgorge into the general world.

This is an astonishing outburst and not quite in character. It looks as though Shakespeare himself had for a moment lost his equanimity and that his heavenly patience with all sorts and conditions of men was ruffled. Nor is this to be wondered at. The fellow who on the score of his own small unfounded grievances against the world rails against all mankind would be least congenial to our author. Be this as it may, the clue is not to be missed. Jaques is here denounced by the one man in the play who takes any real pleasure in his company.

These reactions of Orlando, Rosalind and the Duke, however, are but confirmations of the test applied by Shakespeare in the encounters of Jaques with Touchstone. The relations between the pair are unobtrusively maintained throughout the play. When Jaques, in search of someone from whom to suck melancholy as a weasel sucks eggs, follows Touchstone and Audrey through the forest and overhears their conference, Touchstone, though Jaques has laughed sans intermission an hour by his dial, does not even remember his name—or affects not to remember it. 'Good-even, good Master What-ye-call 't' is his greeting. Touchstone, in fact, is as indifferent in his dealings with Jaques as Jaques is eager to improve the acquaintance. For Jaques, Touchstone is a collector's piece—*un objet d'art et de vertu*. He introduces him to the Duke with a 'Good my lord, give him welcome: this is the motley-minded gentleman that I have so often met in the forest; he hath been a courtier, he swears'. Touchstone plays up to Jaques in their last as in their first encounter. He gives the Duke, as we have noted, a taste of his quality. Jaques plays the part of a delighted *compère*, showing off the paces of the fool like a circus master, prompting him to perform worthily before company and not to let his sponsor down. '*Good my lord, like this fellow. . . . Is not this a rare fellow, my lord? He's as good at anything and yet a fool.*' And

the cream of the jest is that Jaques casting himself for the part of
exhibitor is really the exhibitionist. Touchstone is only too willing to
give the Duke a run for his money but pays not the slightest attention
to Monsieur Melancholy.

But what of the seven ages of man? They too serve the double
purpose. The speech is good hearing. It holds the stage and lingers in
the memory. It is the most successful example of sententious commonplace declamation in English literature. At the same time it
exposes the speaker for what he is and puts a final touch to his
character. It is a good summary of life lived on the average. It has no
depth, not a touch of magic, no suggestion of anything beyond its
narrow limits; and it is coloured throughout by the bilious disposition of the orator. The infant mewls, the schoolboy whines, the lover
sighs, the soldier swears, the judge proses, the pantaloon shrinks and
the old man loses his teeth. Nor is there any indication anywhere
that anyone has truly striven, aspired, suffered, meditated or seen
beyond the end of his nose.

'As You Like It' has been the least fortunate in its critics of all the
plays of Shakespeare. It has often been injudiciously praised—or
scandalously dispraised—for its obvious merits to the neglect of its
finer qualities. Shakespeare in this play brought off two achievements on two different lines of appreciation. The first was to present
his native Arden, to show us true love running happily to a foregone
conclusion (no easy matter), to convey in his own sweet idiom the
pastoral pleasures of woodland and sheep-cote, to moralise agreeably
on the changes of fortune and the simple life—in a word to give us a
sample of the pastoral-comical stripped of its more elaborate affectations. This part of his task he performed so well that it has been
praised with eloquence and propriety by many critics who are content to look no further.

Shakespeare's second achievement has been obscured by the
success of his first. The charming, life-like, conversible comic figures
of the story have been too easily accepted at their own valuation.
The gentle irony that plays about them and their relationships, the
constant reference of character, conduct and environment to the test
of nature, the poise maintained in every scene between permitted

romance and prohibitive reality—these often tend to be partly mis-
conceived or wholly ignored.

The case of Jaques is exemplary. No character in the play is more
consistently put down but he nevertheless imposes upon actors and
spectators alike. 'The prince of philosophic idlers; his only passion is
thought', exclaimed the great Hazlitt of a person whose 'philosophy'
betrayed him into an ecstasy of admiration of a fool's parody—

> And thus from hour to hour we ripe, and ripe,
> And then from hour to hour we rot, and rot—

and whose 'thought' never once emerges above the commonplace.

But Jaques was almost bound to impose on the romantics. The
melancholy man of the Renaissance, a figure of fun at the beginning
of the sixteenth, was a serious literary incubus at the beginning of the
nineteenth century. The romantic critics saw Jaques through a mist
of sorrowful Werthers, itinerant Childe Harolds and mysterious
Manfreds. They were making ready for an orgy that culminated in
the neo-gothic masterpieces of Victor Hugo and the rosicrucian
imbecilities of Lord Lytton. They could no more think of smiling
at Jaques than a devout Anglican would think of laughing in church.
'Son œil est encore vif et beau; mais sa bouche est une tombe où le
sourire est enseveli . . . Au fond de ses récriminations contre le genre
humain, je vois toujours briller l'amour du vrai et la haine du mal,
comme les étoiles derrière les nuages sombres.' The author is George
Sand who in the nineteenth century adapted Shakespeare's play to
the taste of her own time and country. Jaques becomes the active and
ubiquitous hero of the comedy. Fascinated by Monsieur Melancholy
she has little or no time to spare for heavenly Rosalind. Jaques must
show himself at court as well as in the forest, masterly in action as
well as profound in speculation, and in the end be redeemed for
happiness when Celia swears that she loves him by the roses of
spring, the virginity of lilies, by youth, by faith and by honour.

The play is worth reading. It shows what may happen to an Arden
without Touchstone for a guide, counsellor and friend.

III

SHYLOCK

The Merchant of Venice

THE political career of Thomas Devereux, Earl of Essex, frequently impinges upon the dramatic career of Mr. William Shakespeare. In 1593 this proud, capricious, brilliant and foolish nobleman was stimulating the Queen's commissioners to suppress the 'School of Night'. This affair elicited from Shakespeare the first of his notable comedies, 'Love's Labour's Lost'.[1] Eight years later, in 1601, the friends of Essex conspired to stage a revival of 'Richard II', the first of Shakespeare's great tetralogy of histories, which resulted in at least one member of the audience being hanged.[2] Meanwhile, in June 1594, Essex was actively concerned in the persecution of one, Roderigo Lopez, a Jew of Portuguese descent, physician to the Queen, wrongfully accused of plotting to poison Her Majesty for reasons that have ceased to have any great interest for posterity. Essex, who manufactured the evidence, also presided at the trial, an arrangement which greatly simplified the procedure. The unfortunate Jew was hanged, drawn and quartered at Tyburn in the presence of an excited crowd who marvelled that he should dare, in his last moments, to utter the name of Jesus.

The trial and death of Roderigo Lopez was the second *cause célèbre* in a twelvemonth which had for Shakespeare a personal and professional interest. Marlowe and Kyd had been involved in the scandal which led to the suppression of the 'School of Night'. The death of Lopez came yet nearer home. It is not unlikely that Shakespeare was personally acquainted with the man. Lopez, a member of the College of Physicians, was the medical attendant of many notable persons, including the Earl of Leicester, patron of the Company of 'servants and players' in which Shakespeare was a 'sharer'. It is not

---

[1] See above, p. 24.
[2] See the present author's *Political Characters of Shakespeare*, pp. 119, 120.

improbable that Shakespeare witnessed the butchery at Tyburn. Quite certainly he heard the case discussed in the taverns of London, where the lamentable theme of Jewry's place in a Christian commonwealth must have been frequently debated among the free spirits of the time. It is not suggested that Shakespeare, in portraying Shylock, had any political or social intentions. 'The Merchant of Venice' is not a transcript from contemporary life, still less a political morality. It is essentially a fairy-tale or, more precisely, a combination of two fairy-tales. Whether Burbage, in playing Shylock, trimmed his beard to the cut of Lopez or whether the spectators who witnessed the trial of Shylock before the Duke of Venice were prompted to remember the trial of Lopez before the Earl of Essex, is neither here nor there. Gratiano when he declares in his speech to Shylock:

> Thy currish spirit
> Governed a wolf, who hanged for human slaughter,
> Even from the gallows did his fell soul fleet,
> And whilst thou layest in thy unhallowed dam,
> Infused itself in thee

may or may not have been punning on the name Lopez (Lopez= Lupus= Wolf). It is a point for the scholars and we may feel with Horatio when invited by Hamlet to trace the noble dust of Alexander, till he find it stopping a bung-hole, that ' 'twere to consider too curiously, to consider so'. What really matters is the effect on Shakespeare's imagination of this particular fragment of personal experience. He was the likelier, if he had known a Jew with more than one fair daughter (Lopez had three), to find a place for Jessica in his play and to insist, if he had witnessed the savage spectacle at Tyburn, that a Jew, if you prick him, will most certainly bleed. Nor was he likely to forget the indignant mirth of a Christian mob execrating a Jew who in his last agony presumed to call upon Jesus Christ.[1]

[1] That Shakespeare had Lopez in mind when he set out to portray Shylock is incidentally confirmed by the lines that slip into the mouths of Bassanio and Portia at Belmont. Lopez, prior to his prosecution by the Crown, made some damaging admissions concerning the plot of which he was accused, but pleaded at his trial that he had much belied himself in his confession *to save himself from racking*. The use

The Elizabethan theatre reflected the life and mind of the nation and, when Shakespeare sat down to write 'The Merchant of Venice' in 1594, anti-semitism was in fashion. Marlowe had exploited it four years previously with all the resources of his poetic genius and there seemed little more to do or say. Barabbas, the Jew of Malta, embodied in his wicked person all the qualities which a persecuting majority commonly attributed to its victims. For four years Marlowe's Jew had held the stage and, during the excitement aroused by the trial of Lopez, between May and December, 1594, his play was twenty times revived. Barabbas was greedy as a pike, cruel as a cat and artful as a wilderness of monkeys. He was sinister and yet ridiculous, impressive in the intensity of his passion and grotesque in the versatility of his performance. He was robbed of one fortune by the State, but remained master of another. He contrived that two Christian suitors for the hand of his daughter should kill one another; and, when his daughter became a Christian, he killed her, too. He strangled a monk and poisoned a whole nunnery. He betrayed the Christian to the Turk and the Turk to the Christian. Finally he fell into a cauldron which he had artfully contrived for his principal benefactor and was boiled alive.

Such was the play about a Jew which held the London stage when Shakespeare was asked to supply his company with another. Charles

of torture to obtain evidence was a legally respectable institution under Elizabeth; but we need not necessarily conclude that normally decent people regarded it as morally defensible or even a sensible practice. It has always been the habit of English citizens individually to question or condemn proceedings and institutions which for some strange reasons they tolerate or even applaud collectively. Shakespeare's personal views on men and things rarely disturb or colour his imaginative presentation of a character or a situation; but they may be occasionally inferred from a casual epithet or metaphor. There is no reason why Shakespeare, when Bassanio is professing his love for Portia, should suddenly think of the rack. The metaphor just occurs to him because it stood for something freshly present in his mind:

BASSANIO: Let me choose!
               For as I am, I live upon the rack.
PORTIA: Upon the rack, Bassanio! Then confess
        What treason there is mingled with your love.

        Ay, but I fear you speak upon the rack
        Where men enforcèd do speak anything.

Lamb, gazing with aversion upon Barabbas, finds him 'a mere monster brought in with a large painted nose to please the rabble . . . just such an exhibition as a century or two earlier might have been played before the Londoners by Royal Command when a general pillage and massacre of the Hebrews had been resolved on in the cabinet'. Lamb wrote in the comfortable conviction that such exhibitions had ceased for ever to have any relation to practical politics.

Officially there were no Jews in Shakespeare's England. Edward I had driven them all out in 1290. But there was nevertheless a Jewish question, actual as well as legendary, and, in appreciating 'The Merchant of Venice', we shall do well to remember that Marlowe's Barabbas still held the stage when Shakespeare created Shylock. The fashion was fixed and Shakespeare must seem to follow it. It did not matter how absurd or improbable the plot of his play might be, because the public was ready to believe anything about a Jew. Any horrible mischief which a Jew might contrive would be credited and any device by which the Jew might be foiled of his purpose, however childish or improbable, would be commended.

Then why not use that old story of Gernutus, the Jew of Venice, who in merry jest had induced a Christian merchant to sign a bond for a pound of his flesh and who, in cruel earnest, had claimed the forfeiture? This same Gernutus had for some time been a popular figure. There were shortly to be ballads about him, sung to the tune of 'Black and Yellow':

> In Venice town not long ago
> A cruel Jew did dwell,
> Which livèd all on usury,
> As Italian writers tell.
>
> His heart doth think on many a wile
> How to deceive the poor;
> His mouth is almost full of muck,
> Yet still he gapes for more.

Nearer to the purpose were the merry tales of Ser Giovanni Fiorentino, one of those Italian books that sold in Elizabethan England like hot cakes, so that Schoolmaster Ascham was moved to warn his pupils: 'These be the enchantementes of Circes, brought out of Italie to marre men's manners in England.' Ser Giovanni had the whole story almost ready for the theatre: a Venetian youth who had won the lady of Belmonte, a merchant who supplied the youth with money borrowed from a Jew, the pound of flesh, the notorious quibble whereby the merchant was rescued in court by the lady, in disguise, even the mystification about a ring which she received from her bridegroom as a reward for saving his friend. All the dry bones of Shakespeare's play, except for the caskets, were waiting here for the man who could make them live upon the stage.

Nor was it necessary for Shakespeare to look very far for his caskets. They had been lying about for centuries—genuine antiques, bequests from the Greek monk of St. Saba in Syria which, after appearing in places of less repute, had turned up in the *Gesta Romanorum,* a collection of tales so popular with the Elizabethans that no less than six editions of an English translation were published between 1577 and 1601.

It is doubtful whether Shakespeare was even put to the trouble of combining the story of the pound of flesh with that of the caskets. For in 1579, fifteen years before he wrote 'The Merchant of Venice', the actor and dramatic author, Stephen Gosson, leaving the stage for the pulpit, published a 'pleasant invective against poets, pipers, players, jesters and such like caterpillars of the commonwealth', in which he trounced the abuses of the theatre and referred incidentally to two plays showing at the Bull Tavern. One of these plays, entitled 'The Jew', he describes as 'representing the greediness of worldly chusers and the bloody minds of usurers'. From this it must presumably be inferred that a play had been produced either in 1579 or before that date, in which the casket theme (the greediness of worldly chusers) and the story of the pound of flesh (the bloody minds of usurers) had already been woven into a single piece. Thus it seems hardly possible to avoid the conclusion that Shakespeare, in writing 'The Merchant of Venice', was working from an old play in which every essential feature of his double plot already figured.[1]

[1] Another exasperating example of the way in which the critic who hopes to surprise Shakespeare at work finds the ground removed from under his feet. How

There is no means of assessing the merits of the old play from which Shakespeare very probably derived his comedy. But these fashionable Jew plays were probably all very much alike. Dekker wrote one which has been lost. The illiterate Henslowe alludes in his diary to a 'Venesyon Comoedy' produced in August 1594. Another English Jew play of the period, 'Der Jud von Venedig', has survived in a German text. An English company, strolling on the Continent, performed it before a German audience at Halle in 1611. As in Shakespeare's comedy, a second Daniel comes to judgment. If this, or something like it, was the sort of play which Shakespeare had at his disposal when he wrote 'The Merchant of Venice', we can only marvel at the transformation. For this German manuscript is a bawdy, vulgar and brutal piece of work. The essential features of Shakespeare's plot are there, but the result is what might be expected of an attempt by anyone but Shakespeare to present a fairy-tale in the 'Blue Bird' tradition as a contribution to the secular pastime of baiting the Jew.

There is, of course, another side to the picture. The execution of Lopez, while it gratified the Jew-baiters, seems to have provoked indignation and even a searching of hearts among the more reasonable and sensitive citizens of London. Elizabeth, who believed that Lopez was innocent, at first refused to sign his death warrant. She yielded to popular clamour, stimulated by Essex and his friends, but against her better judgment. The feeling inspired by the execution of Lopez in civilised spectators was much the same as that of the pale, fair Briton observed by Heine at Drury Lane who, at the end of the fourth act of Shakespeare's play, several times exclaimed with tears in her eyes: *The poor man is wronged*. In 1596, two years after the

interesting to study in detail the way in which the story of the caskets is dovetailed into the story of the bond as related by Ser Giovanni, if we could be sure that Shakespeare had really done the work! The dramatist rejects passages in the story of the bond which would be ineffective on the stage and replaces them with material from another source. We admire the craft with which the one theme is grafted upon the other and the sure sense of the theatre which prompted the acceptance or rejection of this or that particular feature. All this would provide valuable indications concerning Shakespeare's method and workmanship. But what if all this preliminary work had already been done before Shakespeare put his quill to paper?

production of 'The Merchant of Venice', a book was published in London entitled 'The Orator', a translation from the French of a collection of model speeches or declamations on subjects of historical or contemporary interest. Moral and legal problems were handled in speeches put into the mouths of advocates arguing for or against a particular case. Among the declamations was one which shows that even in Shakespeare's time opinions were divided on the Jewish question. It is a speech such as Shylock might have made in appealing against the sentence of the Venetian Court. The Jew, very ably and convincingly, puts his judges in the wrong, both on moral and legal grounds. What right have these Christians to deny him his pound of flesh? Do they not themselves condemn their debtors to worse for-feits, 'binding all the body into a most loathsome prison or into an intolerable slavery'? Did not the Romans regard it as 'lawful for debt to imprison, beat and afflict with torments the free citizens'? Debtors who fail to keep their contracts must abide the conse-quences. It is lawful to kill a soldier, if he should come to the wars an hour late, or to hang a thief, though he steal never so little. Is it then so great a matter to take a pound of flesh from one who by breaking his promise has endangered his creditor's solvency and reputation, which to a man of business is more precious than life itself?

The Jew here turns the tables on the Christian and, under the cover of a shrewd defence, carries the war to the enemy. The inclusion of such a homily in a book translated and published in 1596 is convincing proof that Shakespeare, in presenting Shylock to the public in 1594, was not writing for an audience incapable of appreciating the more humane aspects of his comedy.[1]

[1] The legend of the pound of flesh is not, in fact, either by origin or in some of its post-mediæval developments, directed against the Jews. There is no Jew in the earliest European version of the tale as narrated by Herbert, the troubadour, in 1223; and in what is perhaps the most amusing version of all, which purports to be an incident in the life of Pope Sixtus V as narrated by Leti, his fanciful biographer, the tables are turned with a vengeance. For in this account it is the Christian who claims a pound of flesh from the Jew (a situation which some may regard as pos-sibly more agreeable to the facts of history); and the good Pope, with magnificent impartiality, condemns both parties to death: the Christian, for entering into a contract with intent to murder the Jew, and the Jew, for signing a bond which virtually involved him in the crime of suicide.

These, then, are the circumstances in which Shakespeare's comedy stands as a piece of contemporary literature: a topical interest in Jews which had led to the production of several Jew plays on the stage, one of which very possibly combined the story of the pound of flesh with that of the caskets; some lively discussion in the London taverns of the rights and wrongs of a distinguished member of that unhappy race, executed at Tyburn; an audience which expected a stage Jew to be presented as a comical and merciless villain; a possible tendency on the part of more judicious spectators to deplore the barbarity of a public act recently committed and to regard the stage Jew of the period as an inhuman travesty.

Shakespeare, having regard to these circumstances, contrived to write a play in which what the contemporary public wanted to meet a topical occasion was with superb felicity combined with what posterity has accepted on its merits as one of his major achievements as a comic dramatist. Here was the 'mere monster brought in with a large painted nose to please the rabble', claiming his pound of flesh; there were the traditional caskets and here was the lady whose locks hung on her temples like a golden fleece—two fantastical stories, one of them wickedly grotesque and the other prettily fanciful, which had somehow to be brought into harmony with one another and to be presented as humanly credible within the limits of a play. Was ever a more formidable challenge presented to a poet, called on to create a mood and to suggest an environment in which these quaint figures and incidents might be accepted, or to a dramatist, called on to create the characters in which we might believe as beings of a like nature with ourselves? Portia, first to last, is as legendary a figure as Shylock. But these legendary figures behave, within their limits, as recognisable creatures of flesh and blood. Humanity comes creeping, or even breaking, into the composition. The people of the play, within a magic circle drawn by the poet, successfully assert their reality.

Shakespeare has so brilliantly succeeded in this part of his task that the veracity of his characters relative to the play—which is just sufficient to carry his design—has been accepted as absolute. Critics and editors insist on viewing every character and incident in the broad light of common day. Bassanio, legendary Jason of the old story, is removed from the play and, because Shakespeare has made him sufficiently real for his purpose, is discussed as though he were a person whom we should hesitate to invite to dinner. He is charged with being a spendthrift and a gold-digger. He sponges on his best friend and marries for money. Antonio, for all his fine speeches and impressive deportment, is a spineless nonentity; Jessica a heartless minx who robs her father. Each character, removed from its context, is submitted to everyday tests of moral worth and social decorum. Shakespeare, in giving to these people just enough reality to make them humanly credible for the purpose of his story, has succeeded to such good purpose that they are brought to judgment as human beings true for all time or in any place.[1]

The severity of the investigations made from time to time into the conduct of these legendary figures, in the course of which they are submitted to all the tests that common decency and common sense would apply to the ordinary affairs of life, is amusingly illustrated by the observations passed upon the character and proceedings of Bassanio by Sir Arthur Quiller-Couch.[2] Take, for example, Bassanio's request that his friend, Antonio, should finance the expedition to Belmont:

'Tis not unknown to you, Antonio,
How much I have disabled mine estate,
By something showing a more swelling port
Than my faint means would grant continuance;

That, says 'Q', is a mighty fine way of saying that you have chosen to live beyond your income. Then, 'Q' continues, there is some 'windy nonsense about shooting a second arrow after a lost one':

[1] Witness the celebrated outburst of Heine: 'Antonio is a poor-spirited creature, with the heart of a worm, whose flesh is really worth nothing else but to bait fish withal. . . . Bassanio is a downright fortune-hunter; he borrows money to show a more swelling port with and to capture a rich heiress. As for Lorenzo, he is an accomplice in a most infamous burglary and under Prussian law he would have been condemned to fifteen years in the penitentiary. The other noble Venetians, who appear in the scene as the comrades of Antonio, do not seem to hate money very much and for their poor friend, when he is in ill-luck, they have nothing but words.'

[2] In his admirable preface to 'The Merchant of Venice'; New Cambridge Edition.

> In my school-days, when I had lost one shaft,
> I shot his fellow of the self-same flight
> The self-same way, with more advisèd watch,
> To find the other forth, and by adventuring both,
> I oft found both: I urge this childhood proof,
> Because what follows is pure innocence. . . .
> I owe you much, and, like a wilful youth,
> That which I owe is lost—but if you please
> To shoot another arrow that self way
> Which you did shoot the first, I do not doubt,
> As I will watch the aim, or to find both,
> Or bring your latter hazard back again,
> And thankfully rest debtor for the first.

Following this 'windy nonsense' comes a speech which 'Q' describes as 'bad workmanship and dishonouring to Bassanio':

> In Belmont is a lady richly left,
> And she is fair, and, fairer than that word,
> Of wondrous virtues—sometimes from her eyes
> I did receive fair speechless messages. . . .
> Her name is Portia, nothing undervalued
> To Cato's daughter, Brutus' Portia—
> Nor is the wide world ignorant of her worth,
> For the four winds blow in from every coast
> Renownèd suitors, and her sunny locks
> Hang on her temples like a golden fleece,
> Which makes her seat of Belmont Colchos' strand,
> And many Jasons come in quest of her. . . .
> O my Antonio, had I but the means
> To hold a rival place with one of them,
> I have a mind presages me such thrift,
> That I should questionless be fortunate.

Why, demands 'Q', should Bassanio build anything on Portia's speechless messages and why should he 'questionless be fortunate', since he knows perfectly well, but does not tell his friend, that all will depend on his choosing the right one of three caskets—a two-to-one chance that Antonio will ever see his money?

These are very pertinent questions if we insist on applying to Bassanio's conduct everyday tests of logic and morality. But we have to consider not whether Bassanio is or is not a suitable young man to be received by a wise father as an eligible suitor for his favourite daughter, but what Shakespeare is doing for his audience. The dramatist has to get this preposterous story of Antonio's bond to the Jew smoothly and effectively under way. This is a play in which impossible things are to happen and they must appear to happen as naturally as possible. Bassanio inevitably takes a mighty fine way of saying that he has lived beyond his income, since we are to enter a world in which the illusion necessary to carry a romantic plot can only be sustained by persons with a mighty fine way of saying most things. Bassanio's little anecdote about the arrows, seriously considered, may be 'windy nonsense', but nothing could be more conducive to the mood in which we are invited to follow his adventures. It may be singularly inappropriate for a young spend-thrift to use so childish an argument in seeking to persuade a long-headed man of business to invest his money. But the argument is entirely appropriate to the major purpose of the scene. Antonio is *not* essentially a long-headed man of business or the play could never have been written. The anecdote of the two arrows establishes at once the atmosphere of a play in which the values of the market-place, the processes of the law and the questing of a young man after beauty and fortune are to be ingredients in a tall story—one of the tallest stories ever put upon the stage. Bassanio's reversion to his 'schooldays' is from this point of view a stroke of genius. It sets the tone for all that is to follow, which, again to quote Bassanio, is 'pure innocence'. The same pure innocence informs the speech which 'Q' pronounces to be 'bad workmanship and dishonouring to Bassanio'. It is not bad but consummate workmanship. Consider, for example, that reference to Jason which announces at once the legendary quality of Bassanio's adventure. Nor is there any question of dis-honour. Bassanio in effect invites his friend to take a two-to-one risk in helping him to win a lady who, as he surmises, has found him not unpleasing. He is not presenting Antonio with a commercial proposi-tion, but with a sporting chance, and Shakespeare intends his audience to accept all this, with more to follow, as we accept the premises of any tall story in which we can be persuaded to believe for our pleasure if we allow the author to suggest or to dictate the mood in which we look and listen.

Parenthetically it may be observed that Shylock never comes within sight or hearing of Belmont. Shakespeare had two equally preposterous stories to tell in his play. Each has its own setting and atmosphere, in which each is credibly presented. Each would destroy the other if they came together and nothing could be more adroit than the way in which the author, in combining the two plots, keeps them moving upon different planes of illusion and yet contrives to make each serve the purpose of the other by contrast. Belmont with its opulent leisure, its merry conversation, its princely adventurers after love and fortune, echoing with 'those dulcet sounds in break of day that creep into the dreaming bridegroom's ear', where young Jason, if he lose, may make 'a swan-like end, fading in music', presents a world in which it is as impossible to imagine Shylock as to imagine the Prince of Morocco, with his shadowed livery of the burnished sun, coming within a mile of that sober house of Israel from which all sounds of shallow foppery are permanently shut. Yet we are persuaded to believe in them both, and the more devoutly for their difference. Each of them is contrived to create its own illusion. And how each of them grips the simple spectator! We follow the choice of the caskets—though we most assuredly know the result—as breathlessly as we follow the turns and twists of the trial. Shakespeare has in each case created conditions in which we suspend all disbelief and are content to hear a story twenty times over without losing interest in the event. He induces in his audience an imaginative suspense in which we identify ourselves with the persons of the tale as distinguished from the cruder suspense of merely wondering what is going to happen next.

Shakespeare's triumph is most marked where probability is most severely strained. The play comes to a climax in the trial scene. Here everything—the laws expounded, the procedure followed, the conduct of the parties, the deportment of all concerned—is, by all normal standards of human conduct, utterly fantastic. This scene, however, has been so carefully prepared, and the mood of the audience is so exactly attuned to receive it, that the case in dispute has been hotly and minutely debated by accomplished lawyers as though it were a serious contribution to the common law of nations. It makes nonsense of every known principle of jurisprudence. It is nevertheless received without misgiving as an authentic leaf from the judicial records of the State of Venice and has become a text for learned Counsel seriously debating the legal issues. Advocates on the one side contend that Shylock was defrauded of his rights by a quibble which no court of law could in decency accept; that Portia, in demanding that a pound of flesh should be cut from Antonio, without shedding a drop of Christian blood, was ignoring an essential principle in the law of contract, since the right to perform a certain act, in this case the cutting of a pound of flesh, confers a right to the necessary incidents of the act, in this case the shedding of blood; that Portia's insistence upon Shylock's cutting exactly a pound, neither more nor less, was legally absurd, since anyone who in law has the right to take a certain amount of anything certainly has the right to take less; that a court which had allowed the legal validity of Shylock's bond could not possibly convict him of a criminal offence for presenting it.

Advocates bringing to bear an equally impressive weight of legal opinion have argued as cogently on the other side. To the plea that, if flesh be removed, blood is implied, it is gravely argued by Portia's advocates that bargains of this nature are to be strictly interpreted and in doubtful points against the party in whose power it lay to make the points of the agreement more explicit; that the sentence in equity is good, though its judicial premises may be irregular; that Portia's victory over Shylock dramatically presents a necessary historic process in the evolution of jurisprudence whereby rigid forms of law inherited from antiquity are brought into harmony with more enlightened conceptions of legal right.[1]

[1] Needless to say these more serious observations are for the most part contributed by German writers.

But nothing quite equals the discovery of a Mr. John T. Doyle, published in 1886, that the procedure followed by the Venetian Court reproduces the essential

E

If Shakespeare, in handling the secondary characters and legal incidents of his play, achieved so strong an illusion of reality that they have been discussed for generations and are still discussed to-day as though he were presenting a transcript from the social life of Venice in the sixteenth century, his delineation of Shylock has had results even more remarkable. He set out to write a comedy about a stage Jew involved in a grotesque story about a pound of flesh. But Shylock, to satisfy his author, must seem to act as a recognisably human being would behave in the given circumstances and Shakespeare has *humanised* him to such good purpose that this comic Jew has become, for many brilliant and sensitive critics, a moving, almost a tragic, figure. Some even go so far as to exclaim of Shylock in his anguish: O what a noble mind is here o'erthrown!

How exactly has this come about? Why and when, if ever, does Shylock cease to be a comic character? Going to Shakespeare's text for an answer to these questions we shall perhaps find a clue not only to the nature of Shakespeare's achievement but to the process by which it is attained.

There is a school of critics which, in reaction from those who discuss Shakespeare's characters as though they were real live persons created without reference to the plays in which they are required to perform certain acts, tend to insist that everything they say or do is determined by some necessity of the plot or technical requirement of the stage. These commentators are often able to show that, where a poet or a psychologist applauds what appears to be a stroke of unfettered genius, the dramatist is merely getting on with what Hamlet called some 'necessary question of the play'. They demonstrate that this soliloquy or that speech, this sequence or that incident, is determined by the mechanics of the Elizabethan stage, by the gifts or limitations of the available actors, by the accepted conventions of the contemporary drama. Then, too, there is always the mere business of keeping the plot in action and putting the characters through such

features of legal practice used in the courts of Nicaragua, with whose Spanish traditions Shakespeare is of course presumed to have been acquainted. For a summary of these legal controversies the reader is referred to twenty pages of notes in the Furness Variorum Edition of the play.

paces as are necessary to that end. A predetermined story has to be told. There is no free-will in the mimic world of the theatre. All we can hope to see is the puppets dallying. Why, for example, should we break our heads over the problem of Hamlet's procrastination? If Hamlet had killed Claudius immediately the play would have come to an end at the close of the first act. Why should we go about to find any special significance in the arrival of Fortinbras when at long last Hamlet lies dead upon the stage? Fortinbras had to enter at that particular moment or there would have been no-one to carry off the bodies, which, in the absence of a curtain, could neither be left merely lying about nor allowed to come alive again and walk off. Maurice Baring has amusingly parodied this approach to Shakespeare, the playwright, in one of his 'Diminutive Dramas', in which Shakespeare, at a rehearsal of 'Macbeth', is sent away to write an extra speech for Burbage, who urges that more effective use should be made of the announcement that the queen is dead. Shakespeare, to Burbage's consternation, obliges with 'To-morrow and to-morrow and to-morrow', which accordingly ceases to be a significant stroke of the poet's genius and may be dismissed as a merely technical concession to the vanity of his leading man.

There is everything to be said in favour of keeping constantly in mind such technical necessities. But to conclude that they limited Shakespeare's creative activity or impaired what was absolute in his characterisation is equivalent to maintaining that the quality and scope of Beethoven's music was determined by the fact that in composing a symphony he accepted limitations of form which required him to state, develop and repeat his subjects in conformity with an approved system of key relationships; or that Bach, in composing 'The Art of Fugue', had, in obedience to technical necessity, no choice but to write precisely the notes which posterity, somewhat tardily, decided to rescue from oblivion as conveying a profound utterance of the human spirit.

There is no better example of interplay between technical craft and creative imagination than the way in which the character of Shylock, apparently predetermined by the necessities of the story in which he figures and by the expectations of the audience to which he was presented, assumes the dimensions and habit of a character which exists freely and in its own right. Admittedly his behaviour in the play is settled in advance. But Shakespeare immediately identifies himself with the sort of person who must inevitably behave in that particular way. Shylock, setting forth upon the stage, is at once a man with hands, organs, dimensions, senses, affections, passions, and the plot to which he must conform soon appears to be no more than an opportunity for bringing him to life. The plot determined the kind of character which Shakespeare created; but the character, once created, determines everything he says or does. It is the paradox of great art that limitations arising from the nature of a given subject, the quality of the materials used and the restrictions imposed by necessary conventions merely serve to concentrate the activity of a free spirit on the business in hand. The artist with little or nothing to express complains of the discipline imposed upon him by the laws of his craft, wastes his energy in quarrelling with his tools or devotes more attention to the invention of a new technique than to the exploitation and development of an inherited tradition. Not so the man of genius. Shakespeare, taking Shylock's merry bond for a theme and accepting all the restrictions of the Elizabethan theatre, expressed himself as freely and profoundly as Beethoven when he unlocked his heart and disclosed the entire length, breadth and depth of his genius, in thirty-three variations on a merry waltz by Diabelli.

Shakespeare in presenting Shylock has so artfully combined the necessities of his plot with the revelation of a character that it is difficult, almost impossible, to say of any single incident or speech which of the two purposes is better served. The man lives in every word that he utters. He has a distinct language of his own and every syllable denotes his quality. His first words are of ducats; his introductory conversation with Bassanio might be cross-headed: Any usurer to any client: *Three thousand . . . ducats . . . For three months . . . Antonio shall become bound . . . Antonio is a good man . . . Yet his means are in supposition . . . The man is notwithstanding sufficient . . . Three thousand ducats—I think I may take his bond.* There is nothing here that seems to serve any other purpose than to present the comic Jew and to get the story under way. But the man is already alive. We shall know him again as soon as he opens his lips—a man whose words are stubborn in his mouth, in whose speech there is no ease or warmth or levity, who hammers out his phrases and can find no way of varying them once they are uttered. *Three thousand ducats . . . Antonio bound.* It is the utterance of a man whose mind is concentrated, obsessed, focused upon a narrow range of fixed ideas. Shylock had the trick of compulsive repetition characteristic of the man in whom imagination, such as it is, forever sits on brood. It is the speech of one who is incapable of humour, whose words will always precisely fit his meaning, in whom no play or flight of fancy is possible:

Ships are but boards, sailors but men. There be land-rats and water-rats, land-thieves and water-thieves—I mean pirates. And then there is the peril of waters, winds and rocks.

Such is the eloquence of Shylock. So literal is his habit of mind that he must interrupt his recitation of the bleak hazards of trade to explain that by water-thieves, a phrase which strikes him as possibly too picturesque to be exactly understood, he means pirates. Contrast with this plain, surly, intensive style of utterance the warm, easy flow of the Venetian gentleman, Salerio, speaking to the same theme:

> My wind, cooling my broth,
> Would blow me to an ague when I thought
> What harm a wind too great might do at sea.
> I should not see the sandy hour-glass run
> But I should think of shallows and of flats,
> And see my wealthy Andrew docked in sand,
> Vailing her high-top lower than her ribs
> To kiss her burial. . . . Should I go to church
> And see the holy edifice of stone,
> And not bethink me straight of dangerous rocks,
> Which touching but my gentle vessel's side
> Would scatter all her spices on the stream,
> Enrobe the roaring waters with my silks,
> And, in a word, but even now worth this,
> And now worth nothing?

Here, then, is Shylock revealed at his first appearance in every phrase that he utters as a certain kind of man and, what is equally to

the purpose, as a totally different kind of man from his Christian
adversaries. His tricks of speech already project a character, unmis-
takeably alive, which will be recognisably true to itself in all that
follows. They will recur throughout the play till they culminate in
those stubborn, reiterated appeals to his bond of a man possessed by
a single thought expressed in a phrase that has become almost an
incantation.

Meanwhile Shakespeare must come immediately to grips with his
story of the comic Jew and the pound of flesh. He grasps the nettle
firmly in an aside wherein Shylock discloses his intention and the
motives behind it:

> How like a fawning publican he looks!
> I hate him for he is a Christian:
> But more for that in low simplicity
> He lends out money gratis, and brings down
> The rate of usance here with us in Venice. . . .
> If I can catch him once upon the hip,
> I will feed fat the ancient grudge I bear him. . . .
> He hates our sacred nation, and he rails,
> Even there where merchants most do congregate,
> On me, my bargains, and my well-won thrift,
> Which he calls interest. . . . Cursèd be my tribe,
> If I forgive him!

There is no hint in this speech, and there has been as yet no suggestion
in the play, that Shylock has any human justification for his monstrous project. For the moment Shakespeare is satisfied with presenting his comic Jew in all the stark, ugly simplicity of the legend with
which his audience was familiar. Shylock detests Antonio because he
is a Christian; because he lends out money gratis and brings down
the rate of usance; because he 'hates the Jews and dislikes their way
of doing business'. Shylock, in this first exhibition of his malice, is a
comic figure and so he remains in the passages that follow: debating
of his present store; delivering the traditional patter of the money-
lender about the difficulty of making up the sum required; justifying
his practice of usury by citing the trick played by Jacob on Laban
over the parti-coloured lambs.

Then comes the first intimation that Shakespeare, having under-taken to supply his audience with a comic Jew committed to a bar-barous enterprise, not only intends to make his conduct psycho-logically credible but has already realised in imagination what it means to wear the star of David:

SHYLOCK: Signior Antonio, many a time and oft
In the Rialto you have rated me
About my moneys and my usances:
Still have I borne it with a patient shrug,
For suff'rance is the badge of all our tribe.
You call me misbeliever, cut-throat dog,
And spet upon my Jewish gaberdine,
And all for use of that which is mine own. . . .
Well then, it now appears you need my help:
Go to then, you come to me, and you say,
'Shylock, we would have moneys'—you say so!
You that did void your rheum upon my beard,
And foot me as you spurn a stranger cur
Over your threshold—moneys is your suit.
What should I say to you? Should I not say
'Hath a dog money? is it possible
A cur can lend three thousand ducats?' or
Shall I bend low, and in a bondman's key,
With bated breath, and whisp'ring humbleness,
Say this:

'Fair sir, you spet on me on Wednesday last—
You spurned me such a day—another time
You called me dog: and for these courtesies
I'll lend you thus much moneys'?

That is perhaps the most remarkable speech in the play. It suggests for the first time on any stage that the Jew has a case. The Jew, more-over, puts that case with a deadly logic, sharpened by persecution to the finest edge, and with a passion which no amount of suff'rance can conceal. It reveals a mind so intensely concentrated upon itself, so constricted in its operation, that it can only express itself in repetitions of a rhythmic, almost hypnotic, quality. *You have rated me*

*about my moneys . . . Shylock, we would have moneys . . . moneys is
your suit. . . . You call me misbeliever, cut-throat dog. . . . Hath a dog
money? . . . You called me dog and, for these courtesies, I'll lend you thus
much moneys. And spet upon my Jewish gaberdine. . . . You that did void
your rheum upon my beard. . . . Fair sir, you spet on me on Wednesday
last.*

Neither in logic nor in passion can Shylock be assailed and the
Christians do not even attempt a rejoinder. Antonio, in fact, calls
down upon himself the doom that awaits one side or the other in any
conflict that passes the bounds of reason:

> I am as like to call thee so again,
> To spet on thee again, to spurn thee too.
> If thou wilt lend this money, lend it not
> As to thy friends—for when did friendship take
> A breed for barren metal of his friend?—
> But lend it rather to thine enemy,
> Who, if he break, thou mayst with better face
> Exact the penalty.

And so we come to the business of the bond. It is a difficult
moment. But note how quickly and easily it is handled. The passages
that precede it may be likened to the patter of a conjurer who dis-
tracts the attention of his audience as he prepares to play his master-
trick. Shylock's speech and Antonio's reply have fixed our attention
on the fundamental issue of the play as between Christian and Jew
and, before we have recovered our emotional balance sufficiently to
realise what is happening, hey presto! the thing is done:

SHYLOCK: Why, look you, how you storm!
              I would be friends with you, and have your love,
              Forget the shames that you have stained me with,
              Supply your present wants, and take no doit
              Of usance for my moneys, and you'll not hear me:
              This is kind I offer.
ANTONIO: This were kindness.
SHYLOCK: This kindness will I show.
              Go with me to a notary, seal me there
              Your single bond, and, in a merry sport,

> If you repay me not on such a day,
> In such a place, such sum or sums as are
> Expressed in the condition, let the forfeit
> Be nominated for an equal pound
> Of your fair flesh, to be cut off and taken
> In what part of your body pleaseth me.

ANTONIO:　　Content, in faith—I'll seal to such a bond,
And say there is much kindness in the Jew.

It is done, too, in a fashion which in no way detracts from the reality of the characters or their relationship. Shylock, in forwarding the plot, is still revealing himself as the kind of man who will later come into court with his knife and scales. There is nothing more sinister-comic in the whole literature of hypocrisy than the two speeches to Antonio. *This is kind I offer. . . . And in a merry sport.* Shylock kind! Shylock merry! Why, even as he makes his proposal, the secret passion that moves him is strong enough to penetrate and subdue his victim who is, as it were, hypnotised into adopting Shylock's own characteristic trick of repetition. 'This were kindness', says Antonio; 'there is much kindness in the Jew.'

The ease with which Antonio is trapped into the bond with Shylock is a good example of the way in which Shakespeare turns to advantage the limitations imposed upon him by his material. Antonio is predestined to sign a contract which will put his life at the mercy of a mortal enemy whom he has every reason to distrust. That is a tall order. Shakespeare does not evade the difficulty, but uses it to serve perhaps the most striking purpose of his play, which is to contrast the narrow, alert and suspicious character of the Jew, member of a persecuted race, with the free, careless and confident disposition of the Christian sure of his place in the sun. It is a contrast maintained in every scene of the play. Shylock in word and deed is typical, intense and precise; the Christians are impulsive, sentimental and wayward. Shylock trusts in his bond; the Christians trust to luck—whether it be Bassanio staking love and fortune on the choice of a casket or Antonio gambling on the ships which fail to come home. Shylock tells us of his 'bargains' and his 'well-won thrift', but riches fall from a window on to the head of Lorenzo. The characteristic qualities on either side are respectively those of the oppressed and the oppressor. If in Shylock we stand appalled by the warping of mind and spirit which oppression inflicts on those who suffer it, we are not less repelled by the infatuated assumption of Antonio and his friends that to them all is permitted in the best of possible worlds. The point is constantly emphasised in the minutest particulars of dialogue and incident. When Shylock, justifying his bargains, cites the case of Jacob and the parti-coloured lambs:

> This was a way to thrive, and he was blest :
> And *thrift* is blessing if men steal it not;

Antonio rejoins:

> This was a venture, sir, that Jacob served for—
> A thing not in his power to bring to pass,
> But swayed and fashioned by the hand of heaven.

Here, incidentally but in a nutshell, the careful husbandry of the Jew is contrasted with the careless genial improvidence of the Christian. Such touches of character, constantly repeated, not only prepare us for Antonio's easy acceptance of the bond but dispose us to swallow the whole preposterous story as entirely natural to the persons conceived.

From the sealing of the merry bond we pass to the story of Jessica. No incident in the play has so richly contributed to the transformation of Shylock, the comic Jew, into a lamentable victim of Christian bigotry and licence. This metamorphosis reached its literary climax in Heine:

I heard a voice with a ripple of tears that were never wept by eyes. It was a sob that could come only from a breast that held in it all the martyr-dom which, for eighteen centuries, had been borne by a whole tortured people. It was the death-rattle of a soul, sinking down dead tired at heaven's gates. And I seemed to know the voice, and I felt I had heard it long ago when in utter despair it moaned out, then as now, 'Jessica, my girl'.

On the stage it attained its theatrical climax, for those who remember it, when Henry Irving returning by the light of a lantern knocked on the door of an empty house. Where, now, is your monster with a large painted nose? This is a patriarch of Israel, wronged in his most sacred affections. Small wonder if, after this, the afflicted Jew grows blind to the quality of Christian mercy.

Alas for those who, seeking to find Shakespeare in one part only of his design, lose or pervert the whole! There is as little warrant for the voice that moaned in Heine's ear as for the Irving interpolation which made of that tragic figure beating on the door a sublime and pathetic incident to wring your hearts.

What are the facts?

Shylock, bidding farewell to his daughter, is more truly comic than at any point of the story so far reached:

> I am bid forth to supper, Jessica.
> There are my keys. But wherefore should I go?
> I am not bid for love—they flatter me.
> But yet I'll go in hate, to feed upon
> The prodigal Christian. Jessica, my girl,
> Look to my house. I am right loath to go—
> There is some ill a-brewing towards my rest,
> For I did dream of money-bags to-night.

This, then, is the voice, the death-rattle of a soul sinking down dead tired at heaven's gates. *Jessica, my girl, look to my house.* Heine, in underlining the pathos, has missed the essential quality of the scene. Shakespeare did not write *'Jessica, my girl'*, but *'Jessica, my girl, look to my house'*, and 'house' is the operative word. In claiming for Shylock the heartbroken misery of a loving father bereft of his child the man of sentiment loses the essential genius of the dramatist who created him. It is the house which stands at the core of Shylock's being; Jessica is no more than the daughter of the house:

> Do as I bid you, shut doors after you:
> Fast bind, fast find.

Not only the doors but the windows must be shut:

> Lock up my doors, and when you hear the drum
> And the vile squealing of the wry-neck'd fife,
> Clamber not you up to the casements then,

> Nor thrust your head into the public street
> To gaze on Christian fools with varnished faces:
> But stop my house's ears, I mean my casements,
> Let not the sound of shallow fopp'ry enter
> My sober house.[1]

Shylock, speaking of his house, is moved almost to poetry. The house is for him a living thing—*Stop my house's ears;* and the word once used, since it stands for one of the few things on which his mind is passionately centred, must be repeated—'*Let not the sound of shallow fopp'ry enter my sober house.*' And that word will be heard again:

> Nay, take my life and all, pardon not that.
> You take my house, when you do take the prop
> That doth sustain my house.

Shylock's farewell to Jessica, which established him for Heine as a tragic figure, leaves him still comic in the play that Shakespeare wrote. Shakespeare has done no more in this scene—but how much it is—than humanise the stage qualities of the comic Jew. Every stroke aims at our sense of comedy. 'Thou shalt not gormandise, as thou hast done with me', he tells Lancelot who is quitting him to serve Bassanio, and, in bidding farewell to this 'huge feeder', he exhibits a malevolence which, like all fixed ideas in a living creature, is at the same time ludicrous and terrible:

> Drones hive not with me.
> Therefore I part with him, and part with him
> To one that I would have him help to waste
> His borrowed purse.[2]

Is Shylock, mourning his daughter's flight, any less comic than

---

[1] Note in this speech a delicious characteristic parenthesis. Having been betrayed into what for his precision is a flight of fancy, he instinctively corrects himself: 'Stop my house's ears, *I mean my casements*'. We have surprised him once before in this same revealing trick of speech when, after talking of water-rats and water-thieves, he felt it necessary to add: 'I mean pirates.'

[2] Let anyone who is disposed to over-sentimentalise Shylock's relations with his daughter ponder his sly warning: *Perhaps I will return immediately.* Distrusting her obedience he cautions her that he may be back sooner than she expects.

Shylock bidding his daughter to shut his doors and windows? A careful study of the scene with Salerio and Tubal provokes conclusions profoundly disconcerting to the heirs of the romantic tradition. It is supremely comic in itself and Shakespeare deliberately contrived in advance that the comic element should prevail over its emotional implications. Far from intending us to sympathise with an afflicted father, he has emphasised before the event that Shylock's affection is abnormally possessive and, in depicting the Jew's reaction to her flight, he subordinates even this self-centred affection to the fury of a man of property upon whose well-won thrift an unspeakable outrage has been committed. *My own flesh and blood to rebel. . . . I say, my daughter is my own flesh and blood.* This chimes perfectly with 'Jessica, my girl, look to my house'. His daughter, his own flesh and blood, has abandoned his house and 'she is damned for it'. She has made off, too, with his jewels and his ducats. There was no need for Shakespeare to introduce this incident at all. It detracts from the pleasure which his audience is clearly intended to take in the sweet infidel who holds a candle to her shames and it encourages romantics and realists alike to take a very poor view of Bassanio's friend, Lorenzo. Heine, as we have seen, would have given Lorenzo fifteen years in the penitentiary. But Shakespeare had other fish to fry. Jessica gilds herself with Shylock's ducats so that Shylock may reveal himself more effectively as an essentially comic character:

SHYLOCK: How now, Tubal! what news from Genoa? hast thou found my daughter?

TUBAL: I often came where I did hear of her, but cannot find her.

SHYLOCK: Why there, there, there, there—a diamond gone, cost me two thousand ducats in Frankfort—the curse never fell upon our nation till now, I never felt it till now—two thousand ducats in that, and other precious, precious jewels. I would my daughter were dead at my foot, and the jewels in her ear! would she were hearsed at my foot, and the ducats in her coffin! No news of them? Why, so—and I know not what's spent in the search: why, thou loss upon loss! the thief gone with so much and so much to find the thief, and no satisfaction, no revenge, nor no ill luck stirring, but what lights o' my shoulders, no sighs but o' my breathing, no tears but o' my shedding. (*he weeps*)

That is admittedly a rather terrible scene. But it is undeniably comic, the victim growing more ludicrous as he becomes more poignantly enslaved to his obsession; and the passage that follows in which Shylock alternately rages at the thought of Jessica squandering his ducats and rejoices to hear of Antonio's losses at sea, brings the comedy to a climax. Shylock's responses to Tubal are like the jerking reflexes of a marionette. They give him just that appearance of a human automaton which is one of the most characteristic effects of pure comedy:

TUBAL: Yes, other men have ill luck too. Antonio, as I heard in Genoa—

SHYLOCK: What, what, what? ill luck, ill luck?

TUBAL: —hath an argosy cast away, coming from Tripolis.

SHYLOCK: I thank God, I thank God! Is it true? is it true?

TUBAL: I spoke with some of the sailors that escaped the wrack.

SHYLOCK: I thank thee, good Tubal, good news, good news: ha, ha! Where? In Genoa?

TUBAL: Your daughter spent in Genoa, as I heard, one night, fourscore ducats.

SHYLOCK: Thou stick'st a dagger in me. I shall never see my gold again—fourscore ducats at a sitting! fourscore ducats!

TUBAL: There came divers of Antonio's creditors in my company to Venice, that swear he cannot choose but break

SHYLOCK: I am very glad of it, I'll plague him. I'll torture him, I am glad of it.

TUBAL: One of them showed me a ring that he had of your daughter for a monkey.

SHYLOCK: Out upon her! thou torturest me, Tubal—it was my turquoise—I had it of Leah when I was a bachelor: I would not have given it for a wilderness of monkeys.

TUBAL: But Antonio is certainly undone.

SHYLOCK: Nay, that's true, that's very true. Go, Tubal, fee me an officer, bespeak him a fortnight before. I will have the heart of him if he forfeit, for were he out of Venice I can make what merchandise I will.[1]

The conclusion is worth noting. Shylock has lost his daughter. He has been wounded to the quick of his personal feeling and racial

[1]As suggested above, this particular passage comes nearer in spirit and treatment to the comedy of Molière than any other scene in Shakespeare. (See Introduction, p. xii).

pride. But Shakespeare still insists on the point from which he started. The Jew hates Antonio because he lends out money gratis and brings down the rate of usance. He will have the heart of Antonio, for 'were he out of Venice I can make what merchandise I will'.

Nevertheless it is this scene from which the romantic tradition of Shylock is mainly derived. For it contains the great speech, so often read and quoted with too little regard for its context, which has misled so many critics into praising Shakespeare as a champion of tolerance and humanity where they might more pertinently have admired his genius as a dramatist and his imaginative intimacy with all sorts and conditions of men:

SHYLOCK: Hath not a Jew eyes? Hath not a Jew hands, organs, dimensions, senses, affections, passions? fed with the same food, hurt with the same weapons, subject to the same diseases, healed by the same means, warmed and cooled by the same winter and summer, as a Christian is? If you prick us, do we not bleed? if you tickle us, do we not laugh? if you poison us, do we not die?

That sounds like a plea for charity. Taken in its context, however, it is something less, and at the same time something more. Shylock's theme is not charity but revenge. He will have Antonio's flesh, if only to bait fish withal:

He hath disgraced me and hindred me half a million, laughed at my losses, mocked at my gains, scorned my nation, thwarted my bargains, cooled my friends, heated mine enemies—and what's his reason? I am a Jew.

and he concludes:

If a Jew wrong a Christian, what is his humility? Revenge. If a Christian wrong a Jew, what should his sufferance be by Christian example? Why, revenge. The villainy you teach me, I will execute, and it shall go hard but I will better the instruction.

Thus, what is commonly received as Shylock's plea for tolerance is in reality his justification of an inhuman purpose. That does not, however, lessen, but rather increase its significance. The most dreadful consequence of injustice is that it degrades not only the oppressor but the oppressed. Shakespeare is concerned to present only the human truth of a situation which he has accepted for the purpose of his play. Shylock, since his motives must be more humanly comprehensible, is presented as a natural product of Christian intolerance, but he does not thereby cease to be a comic character or become an advocate of the humaner virtues. There is something grotesque even in his pleading. *If you tickle us, do we not laugh?* Shakespeare was not here concerned—he never is concerned—with pleading a case in morality. He was presenting Shylock as Shylock lived in his imagination and, in so doing, he showed us how a dramatist, intent only upon his vision, incidentally achieves a moral effect wider in scope and more profound in its implications than a dramatist who consciously devotes himself to an ethical purpose. The comically distorted image of Shylock the Jew is in effect a more telling indictment of Christian oppression, though Shakespeare was not primarily concerned with that aspect of the matter, than the fictitiously sentimentalised presentment of the character created for modern playgoers by Edmund Kean and his successors. Many fine plays have been written by dramatists which expressly indict man's inhumanity to man, but no work of art created with an express political or moral intention is in the last resort so effective, even in the attainment of its purpose, as a work of art which achieves excellence in the form and spirit proper to itself. Critics and actors who, to enhance Shakespeare's hypothetical message, do their best to make Shylock humanly impressive and invite our commiseration for the ruins of a noble nature are likely to discover in the end that they have not only spoiled a comedy but defeated their own object and impaired the moral effect of the play.

There is one other point to be noted in Shakespeare's handling of Jessica. It is often insinuated by commentators who are determined to elevate the issue between Shylock and Antonio, that the Jew was goaded into claiming his pound of flesh by the abduction of his daughter. Here, again, Shakespeare has, in the biblical sense, prevented them. Shakespeare uses the Jessica incident to make Shylock's behaviour in court more acceptable to the audience. We must have seen for ourselves some reason for the Jew's hatred of Antonio made real and visible in dramatic form. Having witnessed the flight of

Jessica and Shylock's reaction to it, we shall be more likely to believe in the inexorable dog who sharpens the knife on his sole. But Shakespeare having used the incident to make the Jew's conduct in court seem less improbable suddenly realises that, in so doing, he may have left us with an impression that Shylock was moved to extremity by paternal anguish, and, as though he foresaw the use to be made of this episode by a romantic posterity, he slips in an explicit repudiation of any such interpretation. When the news of Antonio's arrest reaches Belmont and is discussed with Portia, Jessica assures Bassanio:

> When I was with him, I have heard him swear
> To Tubal and to Chus, his countrymen,
> That he would rather have Antonio's flesh
> Than twenty times the value of the sum
> That he did owe him.[1]

Shakespeare here goes out of his way to inform us expressly that Shylock had made up his mind to kill Antonio long before Jessica's flight with Lorenzo—that he had, in fact, been in the habit of delivering at home speeches of the kind which he was shortly to repeat in the court-house:

> If every ducat in six thousand ducats
> Were in six parts and every part a ducat,
> I would not draw them, I would have my bond!

'Shylock no miser' declared Coleridge in a lecture on Shakespeare delivered on February 6th 1812 to a 'numerous and genteel audience'. He was maintaining that Shakespeare 'drew from the eternal of our nature' and that the miser being but a 'transitory character', peculiar to a certain type of society, could find no place in his imagination. Coleridge would probably have agreed to the obverse of his proposition, namely, that Shakespeare, in depicting a 'transitory character', almost inevitably gave to it a permanent reality. 'Shylock no miser' is a true bill in the sense that he is a man of many parts and qualities. Shakespeare did not, like Jonson, see men as humours walking. He presents us not with character parts or stage types, but with complete

---

[1] This speech of Jessica's incidentally helps us to understand why she had so little compunction about leaving her father's house.

F

and often unaccountable human beings. 'Shylock no miser' is true in
the general sense that he is more than a personification of avarice.
'Shylock no miser' is equally true in the more particular sense that,
though he dreams of money-bags and wishes his daughter hearsed at
his foot with the ducats in her coffin and hates Antonio for bringing
down the rate of usance, he would not for any number of ducats
forgo his revenge on the merchant and refuses thrice the sum due to
him in open court. Shakespeare nevertheless never allows us to lose
sight of the fact that the most *abiding* element in his character is hatred
of extravagance. He may not love money for its own sake, but it
stands for the cardinal virtues in his calendar of sober thrift and
respect for material values. That he should be cheated of his hard-
won bargains by the easy-handed gentlemen of Venice touches him
to the quick. It destroys the very foundations on which he bases his
conduct and assesses his own personal worth. Jessica's behaviour is
an outrage. That she should make away with his ducats is bad
enough. That she should have bartered her turquoise ring—and her
mother's ring at that—for a monkey makes sacrilegious nonsense of
the thrift that in Jacob was blest by the God of Israel.[1]

Shylock makes only one other appearance before his case is heard
and Shakespeare takes this occasion to remind us once again of his
principal grievance against Antonio. The Jew meets him in custody:

> Gaoler, look to him. Tell me not of mercy.
> This is the fool that lent out money gratis.

There is no reference here to a lost child or even to his sacred nation;
and the essentially comic quality of the Jew's mind and utterance,
with its compulsive repetitions, is admirably sustained. The word
'bond' occurs six times:

[1] 'Shylock no miser' inevitably calls to mind Harpagon in Molière's 'L'Avare'.
Molière in his characterisation runs more truly to type than Shakespeare. But the
comic characters of Molière, though they embody more systematically some master
passion of the play, are far from being stage figures with generic labels attached to
them. Molière, like Shakespeare, gets his finest comedy from a conflict of inconsistencies. Shylock, preferring a pound of carrion flesh to thrice three thousand
ducats—one passion driving out another—, recalls Harpagon who in his desire to
cut a figure in the eyes of Mariane, organises a banquet.

I'll have my *bond*, speak not against my *bond*,
I have sworn an oath that I will have my *bond*:
Thou call'dst me dog before thou hadst a cause,
But since I am a dog beware my fangs.

I'll have my *bond*—I will not hear thee speak.
I'll have my *bond*, and therefore speak no more.
I'll not be made a soft and dull-eyed fool,
To shake the head, relent, and sigh, and yield
To Christian intercessors . . .Follow not—
I'll have no speaking, I will have my *bond*.

Shakespeare is now ready—and his audience, too—for the confrontation in court by which his comedy will stand or fall. His task
was to get the maximum dramatic effect out of an intrinsically improbable situation. So well did he succeed that the scene is theatrically
one of the most effective ever put upon the stage. It is, at the same
time, a scene which, owing to the skill with which the playwright
solved his technical problems and brought his characters imaginatively to life as dramatic persons, has moral implications which
exceed the author's immediate purpose. Critics tend to ignore the
technical achievement and make too much of the implications, finding here a noble plea for Christian charity or there an exposure of
Christian barbarity. The court scene is frequently read or produced
as though its prime purpose and title to fame were Portia's very
adequate but by no means outstanding discourse upon the quality of
mercy, whereas, in fact, that speech is merely one of many in which
Shakespeare exploits the dramatic possibilities of the situation.[1]

Shylock, in this scene, achieves his discomfiture by the very
qualities which distinguish him most conspicuously as a comic character. He digs with his own hands the pit into which we know that
he will most assuredly fall and supplies his enemies with the very
weapons by which he is defeated. From the moment in which he
enters the court, he stands inexorably upon the letter of the law.

---

[1] The dramatic significance of this speech lies in its inconsistency with the
behaviour of the Christians who applaud it. From this point of view it may be
regarded as a striking example of the way in which Shakespeare's habit of presenting things as they are constantly reveals the irony of character and circumstance.

The Duke, when the case is opened, entreats him to glance an eye of pity on the losses of Antonio. But Shylock has sworn to have his bond. The Duke asks how he can hope for mercy if he renders none. But Shylock has no need of mercy; Antonio's flesh is dearly bought, 'tis his and he will have it. Portia, finding the bond correct, declares that the Jew must be merciful. But Shylock admits no such compulsion; and, when Portia, echoing the Duke, urges that men should be merciful as they hope for mercy, he exclaims: 'My deeds upon my head, I crave the law.' When Portia begs him to take the money and to forgo the pound of flesh, he charges her by the law to proceed to judgment; he stays upon his bond. The flesh must be cut from the merchant's breast—nearest his heart. So says the bond—those are the very words. Portia asks for a surgeon. But Shylock can find no mention of a surgeon. Is it so nominated in the bond?

Thus, speech by speech, Shakespeare prepares for the moment when Shylock's own insistence upon the letter of the law will be turned against him and when his repudiation of charity will bring its own retribution. Portia's speech on the question of mercy is dramatically merely an item in the comic process.

Note, too, how Shylock increases his own discomfiture—again it is the comic process—by accepting Portia in advance as a worthy representative of the law by which he stands. Portia has been scolded by some critics for keeping the wretched Antonio and his friends on tenterhooks. Surely it was most unkind to bring the poor merchant to the point of baring his breast for the knife when she had it in her power at any moment to shatter the whole case against him.[1] Shakespeare, by lending verisimilitude to this impossible scene, has again betrayed his commentators into applying to it the standards of normal behaviour. He sees to it, as a craftsman, that the scene shall be played for all it is worth and that Shylock shall in every particular

[1] Mr. M. J. Landa in a searching study of the Shylock myth is provoked into a notable outburst on the inhuman conduct of Portia in the trial scene: 'She plays cat and mouse . . . hypocrite to boot.' All this, and much more, equally unanswerable, just shows what happens when we allow ourselves to be misled by Shakespeare's theatrical skill into praising or blaming his characters for conduct which, however true and appropriate in its setting, fails to conform with our standard notions of a good companion.

turn the tables on Shylock. The Jew is self-entrapped not only into supplying the Christian advocate with a plausible justification for strictly rendering the letter of the law against him but into finding for his enemies the very words with which they taunt him in his overthrow. *Most rightful judge! Most learned judge! A Daniel come to judgment!* Portia, proceeding to extremes against Antonio, earns these praises from Shylock in order that they may in poetic justice be used against him. Her behaviour throughout the scene is conditioned by the part which Shakespeare requires her to play in achieving the comic catastrophe.

Shylock is never more Shylock than when he bears the full burden of this incredible scene. He has the same tricks of speech, the same obsessions, the same compulsive habits of thought and expression. The clear stubborn logic of his mind still enables him to confound his enemies by justifying his own practice from Christian example. He has rated Christian hypocrisy—*How like a fawning publican he looks!* He has declared that the Jew, equally with the Christian, knows how to revenge a wrong and can even better the instruction. He now turns in court on the men who counsel mercy and try to argue him out of his rights with the same unanswerable logic:

> You have among you many a purchased slave,
> Which, like your asses and your dogs and mules,
> You use in abject and in slavish parts,
> Because you bought them—shall I say to you,
> Let them be free, marry them to your heirs?
> Why sweat they under burthens? Let their beds
> Be made as soft as yours, and let their palates
> Be seasoned with such viands? You will answer,
> 'The slaves are ours.' So do I answer you—
> The pound of flesh, which I demand of him,
> Is dearly bought, *'tis mine,* and I will have it.

On his own ground, which he claims to share with his persecutors, Shylock is impregnable. He knows, none better, that Christian society is *not* based on the mercy for which the Duke and Portia so ingenuously plead. He asks no more than that the Christians shall apply to his case the principles whereby their own affections and

affairs are ruled. A man may do what he will with his own. Antonio's
flesh is his, legally acquired and dearly bought, and, if he likes to use
it to bait fish withal, that is entirely his affair:

> You'll ask me why I rather choose to have
> A weight of carrion flesh than to receive
> Three thousand ducats: I'll not answer that!
> But say it is my humour, is it answered?
> What if my house be troubled with a rat,
> And I be pleased to give ten thousand ducats
> To have it baned? what, are you answered yet?

He has successfully contrived a situation which enables him to do
for once what they are in the habit of doing every day of their lives
and he means to make good use of it:

> Some men there are love not a gaping pig,
> Some that are mad if they behold a cat,
> And others when the bag-pipe sings i' th' nose
> Cannot contain their urine: for affection,
> Master of passion, sways it to the mood
> Of what it likes or loathes. Now, for your answer:
> As there is no firm reason to be rendered,
> Why he cannot abide a gaping pig;
> Why he, a harmless necessary cat;
> Why he, a woollen bag-pipe; but of force
> Must yield to such inevitable shame,
> As to offend, himself being offended;
> So can I give no reason, nor I will not,
> More than a lodged hate and a certain loathing
> I bear Antonio, that I follow thus
> A losing suit against him! Are you answered?

Shylock, carrying his hatred to extremes, exposes the injustice and
ferocity of the social institutions from which it springs. He appeals
to the twin laws of retribution and property on which the society in
which he lives is based. Nothing is further from Shakespeare's mind
than to convey a lesson. But the lesson is there, product of a perfectly
balanced and sensitive mind intent upon the dramatic presentation of
human realities. The debated question whether Shakespeare writing

certain passages of 'The Merchant of Venice' was pleading for tolera-
tion or indicting Christian hypocrisy, exalting equity above the law
or divine mercy above human justice, does not arise. He presents a
situation in which all these issues are involved, characters in which
their effects are displayed, arguments appropriate to the necessary
incidents and persons of the comedy; and leaves it to his critics to
draw the indictment or convey the apology. His purpose was to
write a comedy and he is never more intent on this purpose than in
the scene whose moral implications have excited so much interest
among those who study the play in the light of their own ethical and
social standards. Shylock eagerly producing the bond for Portia's
inspection—the bond which is to prove his own undoing—is undeniably comic. So is Shylock examining the bond to verify that the
flesh must be cut from Antonio nearest his heart. So is Shylock looking in vain for any mention of a surgeon. So is Shylock applauding
the wisdom of the judge who is about to ruin him. So, above all, is
Shylock promptly asking for the return of his money when he
realises that his claim to Antonio's flesh will not be allowed.

And behind all this obvious comedy is the indifferent irony of the
comic spirit which, in presenting the human realities of a situation,
necessarily exposes the blindness of human beings to their own
inconsistencies: Portia, singing the praises of mercy when she is
about to insist that the Jew shall have the full rigours of justice
according to the strict letter of the law; Antonio, congratulating
himself on his magnanimity in the very act of imposing on his
enemy a sentence which deprives him of everything he values;
Christian and Jew mutually charging one another with an inhumanity which is common to both parties.

How Shylock, imagined by Shakespeare as a comic figure and
sustaining his comic character to the last, was yet able to become a
depositary of the vengeance of his race (Hazlitt), the ruins of a
great and noble nature (Hudson) and the most respectable person in
the play (Heine) is now perhaps sufficiently evident. The question
when and how, if ever, Shylock ceases to be comic answers itself as
we read the play. To the question when? the answer, if we bear in
mind that Shakespeare's comedy springs from imaginative sympathy

and not from intellectual detachment, is: never for an instant. The question how? should not therefore arise. But alas for logic and the categories! No-one can remain wholly insensible to the emotional impact of the play. The imaginative effort expended by Shakespeare in making his Jew a comprehensibly human figure has imparted to him a vitality that every now and then stifles laughter and freezes the smile on our lips. If these passages are rightly handled by the actor or accorded their just place and value by the reader, the comedy remains intact. If, on the contrary, these passages are thrown into high relief and made to stand out of their context, the comedy is destroyed. Heine maintained that Shakespeare *intended* to write a comedy but was too great a man to succeed.[1] This comes very near the truth, but what really happened was something rather more subtle and difficult to describe. Shakespeare took the comic Jew for a theme, and wrote a true comedy. But it was a comedy after his own pattern and desire —a comedy in which ridicule does not exclude compassion, in which sympathy and detachment are reconciled in the irony which is necessarily achieved by the comic spirit in a serene presentation of things as they are.

Shylock as a comic character held the stage for over a century. Then came an interval of forty years, from 1701 to 1741, when good taste imposed on English audiences a mangled version of the play by Lord Lansdowne, a nonentity whose trimmings and embellishments may be recommended to the curious as an upstanding monument to the complacency with which an eighteenth-century nobleman was able to view the achievements of a barbarian:

> The first rude sketches Shakespeare's pencil drew
> But all the shining master-strokes are new;
> This play, ye critics, shall your fury stand
> Adorn'd and rescu'd by a faultless hand.

[1] Heine wrote: 'Shakespeare intended perhaps, for the amusement of the 'general', to represent a tormented, fabulous creature that thirsts for blood, and of course loses his daughter and his ducats, and is ridiculed into the bargain. But the genius of the poet, the genius of humanity that reigned in him stood ever above his private will and so it happened that in Shylock, in spite of all his uncouth grimacings, the poet vindicates an unfortunate sect, which, for mysterious purposes, has been burdened by Providence with the hate of the rabble both high and low, and has reciprocated this hate—not always by love.

Shylock was still a comic character, for whom Lord Lansdowne was good enough to provide fresh occasions for mockery, notably at a banquet where the Jew drinks to his money-bags. Then, in 1741, came Macklin of whom Pope, not without good reason, indited a famous epitaph:

> Here lies the Jew
> That Shakespeare drew.

There is some evidence that it was Macklin who first suggested to an English audience that Shylock was pathetic. 'The Jew's private calamities', says Davies, who saw Macklin at Drury Lane, 'made some tender impressions on the audience'. But Macklin's Shylock was in the comic tradition and it gave birth to a whole generation of comic Shylocks who devoted their considerable talents to building up the grotesque figure denounced by Hazlitt: a 'decrepit old man, bent with age and ugly with mental deformity, with the venom in his heart congealed in the expression of his countenance, sullen, morose, gloomy, inflexible, brooding over one idea, that of his hatred, and fixed on one unalterable purpose, that of his revenge'.[1]

All these Shylocks were destroyed in a single night by Edmund Kean on January 14th, 1741. Kean converted Hazlitt and for the next hundred years Hazlitt's judgment was never seriously challenged. All the great actors conspired to perpetuate and adorn the new reading. The nobility of Macready's Shylock was in due course exceeded by the priestly dignity of Henry Irving (1879) and the aristocratic good form of Forbes Robertson.[2] The actor's triumph over the author was by the end of the nineteenth century complete.

Shakespeare has finished with Shylock when he stumbles from the court:

> I am not well. Send the deed after me
> And I will sign it.

---

[1] See Harold Child's note on the *Stage History of the Play*; New Cambridge Edition.

[2] Within living memory there have nevertheless been notable attempts to restore Shakespeare's comic character to the stage. Sir William Poel, in 1898, conveyed to a modern audience some idea how Shylock comported himself in the Elizabethan theatre, and Mr. Michael Sherbrooke in 1941 bravely insisted that Shylock, even at his most terrible, was essentially ludicrous.

The law which he invoked pursues him to the last, and the bond in which Antonio signed away his life is replaced by the deed in which the Jew must sign away his property. Shakespeare, who has used all his art to put Shylock credibly before our eyes in flesh and blood, now takes us back to the pleasant estate of Belmont which, with a skill that will claim your admiration if you look into it at all closely, he has kept so carefully secluded from the harsh realities of the ghetto and the market-place. We hear the music to which the ears of Shylock's house were closed. Music in Shylock's Venice is a vile squeaking of the wry-necked fife or a bag-pipe that sings i' th' nose. Music at Belmont now enters with moonlight to take entire possession:

> LORENZO: How sweet the moonlight sleeps upon this bank!
> Here will we sit, and let the sounds of music
> Creep in our ears—soft stillness and the night
> Become the touches of sweet harmony.
> Sit, Jessica. Look how the floor of heaven
> Is thick inlaid with patines of bright gold,
> There's not the smallest orb which thou behold'st
> But in his motion like an angel sings,
> Still quiring to the young-eyed cherubims;
> Such harmony is in immortal souls!
> But whilst this muddy vesture of decay
> Doth grossly close it in, we cannot hear it.
>
> The man that hath no music in himself,
> Nor is not moved with concord of sweet sounds,
> Is fit for treasons, stratagems, and spoils,
> The motions of his spirit are dull as night,
> And his affections dark as Erebus:
> Let no such man be trusted.

The little candle in Portia's hall throws its beams; so shines a good deed in a naughty world. We are back in the age of innocence when tales are told indoors by candlelight, and beyond the window, Peace ho, the moon sleeps with Endymion! Here we can believe again in the lucky caskets and are caught up in a pretty confusion of rings and posies. Antonio's ships can now come home and the story of Shylock lingers in the memory as an old, unhappy tale.

But it was a tale in which we believed—and to such good purpose that for generations its rights and wrongs, its arguments and incidents and the persons who figured in it, have been seriously debated as matters pertaining to the 'eternal of our nature'.

IV

BOTTOM

A Midsummer Night's Dream

If he come not, then the play is marred. It is Bully Bottom who, by reason of his special quality, holds firmly together the gossamer structure of that most aery fabric of a vision which is Shakespeare's 'A Midsummer Night's Dream'. It is not a quality to be easily defined. The French have a word for it. Bottom is *débrouillard*—equal to all occasions and at home wherever he may be. Nothing can disconcert or put him down or prevent him from being entirely and happily himself. He wears an ass's head as imperturbably as he bestows advice upon his rustic companions or corrects Duke Theseus for suggesting that Wall should speak out of his cue. He has been rated for conceit and pushing himself forward overmuch. But that is unjust. He engrosses the play not because he is obtrusive, but because he is ingenuously eager to meet all occasions and to throw himself into any part in life that offers. Nor does his love of life exceed his ability to cope with it. He does not unduly press either himself or his suggestions on the company but yields with good grace to the common voice.

He is, in fact, just the man for Shakespeare's purpose. There has to be someone who can be equally at home in each of the three compartments of this trinity of fantastic worlds—classical antiquity, rural Britain and the kingdom of the fairies. Duke Theseus brings home to Athens a mythological bride won with his sword, exercises patriarchal authority over men and maidens, and hunts with hounds bred out of the Spartan kind. Hippolyta, the bride aforesaid, consorted in her maiden days with Hercules and Cadmus. We are here immersed in the legends of ancient Greece—except that round the corner is a convent in which disobedient daughters may be consigned to wither on the virgin thorn. From legendary Athens we are suddenly transported to a village obviously in the heart of Tudor England, where a carpenter, a weaver, a bellows-maker, a tinker, a tailor and a joiner are met together to devise a pastime for the local squire. Finally we pass, without warning given, to a world to whose inhabitants the cowslips are tall and where elves creep into acorn-cups to hide themselves in fear from the chiding of Oberon and Titania.

How does Shakespeare contrive to pass so easily from one of these three compartments of his play to another without disturbing our sense of their mutually destructive realities? Duke Theseus is more than life size; the fairies are minute. In between, like Gulliver alternatively with the Brobdingnagians and the Lilliputians, is the company of Peter Quince. Each group has its own standards of size, quality, sentiment and behaviour. Yet we easily believe in all three at once. Each part confirms the illusion of the whole.

To effect this miracle Shakespeare needs a magician who is none other than Bully Bottom. For Bottom impersonates the quality which puts the poet at the centre of his creation. To Bottom, as to Shakespeare, all these beings, fairy, heroic or human, are equally congenial. Bottom has a welcome ready for all that may betide. He takes everything in his stride of simple, indomitable assurance. His readiness to play the tyrant, the lover, the lady or the lion in the most lamentable comedy and most cruel death of Pyramus and Thisbe enables him, in a wood near Athens, to hold his court as to the manner born among the 'little people', accepting without question the cosseting of Titania and ingenuously confessing to a great desire for a bottle of hay.

In no other play is Shakespeare's skill in weaving one harmonious design of several strands more notable. The three themes are contrasted, but there is an underlying unity between them. We pass from key to key, but the keys are related and the modulations from one to another contrived with a disarming simplicity. Unity of mood and texture is established by a certain quality of innocence that runs through all. The Athens of Duke Theseus, where fathers are as gods to their children, where Hippolyta's moon is like to a silver bow new-bent in heaven, where the court rises early to observe the rite of May, takes us back to that golden world to which poets of the Renaissance so often reverted. To this primitive world belong

Hermia and Lysander who fly to the wood; Helena who 'tells on' her friend, the rival gallants who breathe love, contempt, fire and slaughter as occasion prompts, and the little, fierce maid who was a vixen when she went to school:

> Your hands than mine are quicker for a fray,
> My legs are longer though to run away.

These be nursery humours, as Corporal Nym would say. The tale of Theseus and his bouncing Amazon, of the moonstruck gallants in the wood and Titania's theft of the little changeling boy—all is silly sooth

> And dallies with the innocence of love
> Like the old age.

From a ball in the palace of Duke Theseus to a room in the cottage of Peter Quince is accordingly no such distance as it seems. For here, too, is a simplicity of the same pristine quality and it is easy going from one to the other.

To pass thence into the kingdom of Oberon is a more hazardous journey. But the mood is still pure innocence. These fairies are the simplest of creatures. They are of a world which has not yet grown up. Robin Goodfellow's idea of a jest is of same order as Bottom's delight in roaring like a lion:

> And sometimes lurk I in a gossip's bowl,
> In very likeness of a roasted crab,
> And, when she drinks, against her lips I bob,
> And on her withered dewlap pour the ale.
> The wisest aunt, telling the saddest tale,
> Sometime for three-foot stool mistaketh me:
> Then slip I from her bum, down topples she,
> And 'tailor' cries, and falls into a cough.

Oberon and Titania make much of their jealousy, but it is jealousy for a plaything. The fairies steal honey-bags and pluck the wings from painted butterflies. Oberon slips from fairyland to play on pipes of corn or listen to the song of a mermaid. Titania is sung to sleep with a lullaby while a sentinel stands on guard to drive away spotted snakes, thorny hedgehogs, newts, spiders, blackbeetles, worms and snails. These fairies provoke the critic to excel himself in dainty epithets such as trim, pretty, elegant, graceful, comely. Their hardest labour is picking apricots and dewberries; their sport is killing a red-hipped humble-bee on the top of a thistle; their pleasure is dancing ringlets to the whistling wind or singing a roundelay by firelight through a silent house when everyone else is in bed. It is the golden age of Theseus in miniature and the commentator, grown solemn, is moved to observe that in these little lives there are no attributes of the properly natural and moral soul, nothing of reason or conscience in their felicity.

Observe how the composer of this little symphony moves from key to key.

Note for example how he prepares us in the Duke's palace to accept the amative caprices of a wood near Athens. Lysander wooing Hermia with knacks and nosegays, with trifles and gauds, has 'stolen the impression of her fantasy'. Love, which is to spring alive or vanish at the touch of a magic herb, is already half childish and three parts fanciful:

> Love looks not with the eyes, but with the mind:
> And therefore is winged Cupid painted blind.
> Nor hath Love's mind of any judgment taste:
> Wings and no eyes figure unheedy haste.
> And therefore is Love said to be a child:
> Because in choice he is so oft beguiled.

Demetrius is 'this spotted and inconstant man' before ever he falls a victim to Puck's mischief. It needs no fairy come from the grove to tell us that young lovers can be fickle and young love itself

> Momentany as a sound,
> Swift as a shadow: short as any dream;
> Brief as the lightning in the collied night,
> That, in a spleen, unfolds both heaven and earth;
> And ere a man hath power to say 'Behold!'
> The jaws of darkness do devour it up:
> So quick bright things come to confusion.

Shakespeare is singing us into the mood in which we shall accept without question the magic of Oberon and his little western flower, whose liquor—

> on sleeping eyelids laid,
> Will make or man or woman madly dote
> Upon the next live creature that it sees—

and, having sung us into the mood where Titania rounds the hairy temples of an ass with a coronet of fresh and fragrant flowers and where four human lovers are bewitched into preposterous confusions and rivalries, he sings us out again in the measured accents of Theseus:

> Lovers and madmen have such seething brains,
> Such shaping fantasies, that apprehend
> More than cool reason ever comprehends.
> The lunatic, the lover, and the poet
> Are of imagination all compact.
> One sees more devils than vast hell can hold;
> That is, the madman. The lover, all as frantic,
> Sees Helen's beauty in a brow of Egypt.
> The poet's eye, in a fine frenzy rolling,
> Doth glance from heaven to earth, from earth to heaven;
> And as imagination bodies forth
> The forms of things unknown, the poet's pen
> Turns them to shapes, and gives to airy nothing
> A local habitation and a name.

More subtle is his modulation from the dream in 'A Wood near Athens' to the illusion of broad Athenian daylight. Oberon disenchants the eyes of Titania, and Puck takes from Bottom the ass's head. Elves tread a measure till Puck hears the morning lark, and Oberon remembers Theseus. The fairies vanish to follow after the shades of night and their voices fade into a music of horns heard distantly. The Duke with his foresters comes 'in the vaward of the day' to speak of hounds with 'ears that sweep away the morning dew'. The horns which first announced the new key now establish it firmly, being blown again of set purpose to awaken the sleeping lovers, and the modulation is complete.

But Bottom still lies sleeping in the sun—no longer an ass or a queen's consort in fairyland but Nick Bottom, the weaver, who must find his way back to the city. Still half-asleep, he calls aloud for his friends and fellow-players in the interrupted rehearsal. His mind is still full of his marvellous adventure and he dwells in wonder upon his 'translation', but his thoughts turn instinctively to his companions of middle earth. And what a story he has to tell! *Spread yourselves, masters.* Again the new key is established. Bottom is himself again:

BOTTOM (*awaking*): When my cue comes, call me, and I will answer. My next is, 'Most fair Pyramus'. Heigh-ho . . . Peter Quince! Flute, the bellows-mender! Snout, the tinker! Starveling! God's my life! stol'n hence, and left me asleep! I have had a most rare vision. I have had a dream—past the wit of man to say what dream it was. Man is but an ass, if he go about to expound this dream. Methought I was—there is no man can tell what. Methought I was, and methought I had . . . but man is but a patched fool, if he will offer to say what methought I had. The eye of man hath not heard, the ear of man hath not seen, man's hand is not able to taste, his tongue to conceive, nor his heart to report, what my dream was. I will get Peter Quince to write a ballad of this dream: It shall be called Bottom's Dream; because it hath no bottom.

Just as in music the return to an old key has on the ear an effect of difference, so these lovers awakened by the horns of Theseus, and Bottom emerging from his dream, bring back with them a sense of all that has gone before to colour this repetition of themselves.

DEMETRIUS: These things seem small and undistinguishable,
            Like far-off mountains turnèd into clouds.
HERMIA: Methinks I see these things with parted eye,
            When everything seems double.
HELENA: So methinks:
            And I have found Demetrius like a jewel,
            Mine own, and not mine own.
DEMETRIUS: Are you sure
            That we are awake? It seems to me
            That yet we sleep, we dream. Do not you think
            The duke was here, and bid us follow him?
HERMIA: Yea, and my father.
G

Bottom, though glad enough to be back with his friends, is full to the brim with wonders, drenched in the fragrance and magic of an experience which he is bursting to share with all and sundry, but which, he knows, can never be imparted:

BOTTOM: Where are these lads? where are these hearts?
QUINCE: Bottom! O most courageous day! O most happy hour!
BOTTOM: Masters, I am to discourse wonders: but ask me not what; for if I tell you, I am not true Athenian. I will tell you every thing, right as it fell out.
QUINCE: Let us hear, sweet Bottom.
BOTTOM: Not a word of me. All that I will tell you is, that the duke hath dined.

Let us now come closer to this most lovely, gentlemanlike man and consider in some detail his part in the comedy.

We meet him first at the house of Peter Quince and, be it noted at once, Peter Quince is master of the company. It is Quince who has chosen the play, called the players together and assigned them their parts. Bottom accepts his authority and never questions his decisions. For Bottom, though prolific in advice, fancying himself in all parts, is neither envious nor pushful, but just immensely eager to get things done. Quince is obviously no leader of men. He needs counsel and support:

First, good Peter Quince, say what the play treats on: then read the names of the actors: and so grow to a point. . . . Now, good Peter Quince, call forth your actors by the scroll. . . . Masters, spread your-selves.

And so grow to a point. But Bottom, nudging forward his less ardent companions, is betrayed into holding up the proceedings by the very qualities which make him so helpful and necessary—sheer enthusiasm, good-fellowship, an unfailing readiness to meet all occasions and to identify himself with all sorts and conditions of men. He is set down for Pyramus, a lover that kills himself, most gallant, for love. Bottom sees himself at once in the part. It will ask some tears in the true per-forming of it and let the audience look to their eyes. He will move storms. He will condole in some measure. But his chief humour is for a tyrant. He could play Ercles rarely or a part to tear a cat in, to make all split. Note, however, that in full flight after his crowding fancies Bottom pulls himself up, not once but repeatedly. 'To the rest', he interjects, motioning Quince to proceed. 'Now name the rest of the players', he urges a moment later. But presently he is off again. He would play Thisbe, too, and speak in a monstrous little voice. Quince checks him in mid career. Bottom must play Pyramus, and Flute Thisbe. 'Proceed', says Bottom. But the lion is too much for his self-control. Lover, lady or lion—he sees himself equally well in all three. Quince begins to be put out by all this enthusiasm. He tactfully objects that Bottom is likely to play the lion only too well:

BOTTOM: Let me play the lion too. I will roar, that I will do any man's heart good to hear me. I will roar, that I will make the duke say, 'Let him roar again: let him roar again.'

QUINCE: An you should do it too terribly, you would fright the duchess and the ladies, that they would shriek: and that were enough to hang us all.

ALL: That would hang us, every mother's son.

BOTTOM: I grant you, friends, if that you should fright the ladies out of their wits, they would have no more discretion but to hang us: but I will aggravate my voice so, that I will roar you as gently as any sucking dove: I will roar you an 'twere any nightingale.

QUINCE: You can play no part but Pyramus: for Pyramus is a sweet-faced man; a proper man as one shall see in a summer's day; a most lovely, gentlemanlike man: therefore you must needs play Pyramus.

BOTTOM: Well . . . I will undertake it.

Bottom's imagination, now focused upon Pyramus, prompts him to raise the question of make-up—a matter of passionate interest to all who engage in amateur theatricals:

BOTTOM: What beard were I best to play it in?

QUINCE: Why, what you will.

BOTTOM: I will discharge it in either your straw-colour beard, your orange-tawny beard, your purple-in-grain beard, or your French-crown-colour beard, your perfect yellow.

Dr. Johnson, who is very severe on Bottom, regards this passage as a deliberate satire upon the 'prejudices and competition' of players. 'Bottom, who seems bred in a tiring-room, is for engrossing every part and would exclude his inferiors from all possibility of distinction. . . . Here, again, he discovers a true genius for the stage by his solicitude for propriety of dress and his deliberation which beard to choose among many beards, all natural.' But where is the evidence that Bottom would exclude his inferiors? And is he for engrossing every part? He certainly enjoys *the idea of himself* in any part that life or the stage may offer, but that is not at all the same thing. Shakespeare has much more in hand than a satire upon the prejudices and competition of players. He is establishing a character who is shortly to play such a part as has not yet entered into the tongue of man to conceive nor his heart to report. Bottom's interest in beards is shared by any villager who undertakes to figure in a local pageant and it is expressed in terms such as would be used quite naturally by a weaver with a professional interest in the dyes of his craft.

Peter Quince's theatrical company arrange to meet at the Duke's oak in Palace Wood. It is a marvellous convenient place for a rehearsal—this green plot shall be our stage, this hawthorn-brake our tiring-house. Here the conversation turns upon the nature of dramatic illusion, which, if Hazlitt is to be trusted, Bottom 'seems to have understood at least as well as any modern essayist'. Hazlitt, by the way, finding subtle differences between the parties to this conversation, enlarges here on what he describes as the *accidental* felicities of Shakespeare. 'It is too much to suppose all this intentional', he writes, 'but it very luckily falls out so. Nature includes all that is implied in the most subtle analytical distinctions'—an observation which is not only relevant to this present analysis of imponderables but might with propriety be inscribed upon the fly-leaf of any critical study which sets out to find reason and method in achievements attained by the more simple process of intuition.

Bottom, immersed in the most lamentable comedy of Pyramus and Thisbe, fears that his audience may mistake this mimic world for reality. He must draw a sword to kill himself, which the ladies cannot abide. He has given much thought to the matter and, being Bottom, he has a simple device to make all well:

Write me a prologue, and let the prologue seem to say—we will do no harm with our swords, and that Pyramus is not killed indeed: and, for the more better assurance, tell them that I, Pyramus, am no Pyramus, but Bottom the weaver: this will put them out of fear.

Then, too, there is still that difficulty about the lion:

BOTTOM: Masters, you ought to consider with yourselves—to bring in (God shield us!) a lion among ladies, is a most dreadful thing. For there is not a more fearful wild-fowl than your lion living; and we ought to look to 't.

SNOUT: Therefore, another prologue must tell he is not a lion.

BOTTOM: Nay: you must name his name, and half his face must be seen through the lion's neck, and he himself must speak through, saying thus, or to the same defect: 'Ladies,' or 'Fair ladies—I would wish you', or, 'I would request you', or, 'I would entreat you, not to fear, not to tremble: my life for yours. If you think I come hither as a lion, it were pity of my life. No: I am no such thing: I am a man as other men are' . . . and there indeed let him name his name, and tell them plainly he is Snug the joiner.

Finally, there is the question of how to bring moonlight into the chamber. Snout is all for plain realism. Doth the moon shine that night? Bottom, quick on the scent of any promising idea, calls for a calendar. Find out moonshine, find out moonshine! The calendar is propitious and Bottom, eagerly helpful, observes that the moon may shine in at the great casement. But Quince is no realist. Nature is all very well, but the theatre has its own properties and devices. Let someone enter with a bush of thorns and a lanthorn to present the person of Moonshine. Bottom, as quick to adopt the symbolical as the naturalistic view, not only accepts this suggestion but applies it to the solution of the problem how to bring a wall into the great chamber:

Some man or other must present wall: and let him have some plaster, or some loam, or some rough-cast about him, to signify wall; and let him hold his fingers thus . . . and through that cranny shall Pyramus and Thisbe whisper.

So ends the simple colloquy on that suspension of disbelief which philosophers have stated to be necessary to the creation of dramatic illusion. There is perhaps something to be said for Hazlitt's contention that Bottom understood the matter as well as any man before or since.

And so, having discoursed upon the problem of reality in art and nature, Bottom retires into the hawthorn-brake. There he awaits a cue for Pyramus and returns to 'the green plot which is our stage' transformed into an ass. His companions, who have just considered with themselves how dreadful a thing it is to bring in a lion among ladies, are now confronted with a yet more fearful illusion and there is here no actor with half his face seen through the ass's neck to assure them that he is but a man as other men are. They flee, one and all, from this fearful wild-fowl and Bottom is left 'translated' to face his great adventure alone:

I see their knavery. This is to make an ass of me, to fright me if they could: but I will not stir from this place, do what they can. I will walk up and down here, and will sing that they shall hear I am not afraid.

The song which awakens the Queen of the Fairies is not unworthy:

> The ousel cock, so black of hue,
>   With orange-tawny bill,
> The throstle with his note so true,
>   The wren with little quill.

Bottom is neither to be flustered nor flattered. He has an unerring sense of the fitness of things which never deserts him—a quality which no self-centred, conceited person—as he is so unfairly charged with being—could possibly have exhibited in such a situation. Here is a fairy queen protesting that she loves him, voice, shape, virtue, intelligence and all. It is a little staggering, disconcerting alike to his modesty and good sense; but Bottom does not lose his presence of mind:

BOTTOM: Methinks, mistress, you should have little reason for that. And yet, to say the truth, reason and love keep little company together now-a-days. The more the pity, that some honest neighbours will not make them friends. Nay, I can gleek upon occasion.

TITANIA: Thou art as wise as thou art beautiful.

BOTTOM: Not so, neither: but if I had wit enough to get out of this wood, I have enough to serve my own turn.

Titania declares that he shall stay with her whether he will or not. She is a spirit of no common rate and promises him fairies to do his pleasure. Bottom is silent but his silence is gracious. Who would interrupt such fairy talk as falls from the lips of Titania?

> Be kind and courteous to this gentleman,
> Hop in his walks and gambol in his eyes,
> Feed him with apricocks and dewberries,
> With purple grapes, green figs, and mulberries.
> The honey-bags steal from the humble-bees,
> And for night-tapers crop their waxen thighs,
> And light them at the fiery glow-worm's eyes,
> To have my love to bed and to arise,
> And pluck the wings from painted butterflies,
> To fan the moonbeams from his sleeping eyes.
> Nod to him, elves, and do him courtesies.

But these fairies who come to wait upon him must be answered. Bully Bottom, who, like his author, takes all things in nature as they come, is put upon his mettle. And how featly he rises to the occasion, with nothing but his native good-fellowship and genial acceptance of things as they are to carry him through. For each of them he has an appropriate word. He holds his court with an exquisite, royal courtesy that stoops, without pride, to claim equality with his lieges:

PEASEBLOSSOM: Hail, mortal!
COBWEB: Hail!
MOTH: Hail!
MUSTARDSEED: Hail!
BOTTOM: I cry your worships mercy, heartily; I beseech your worship's name.
COBWEB: Cobweb.
BOTTOM: I shall desire you of more acquaintance, good Master Cobweb: if I cut my finger, I shall make bold with you. Your name, honest gentleman?
PEASEBLOSSOM: Peaseblossom.
BOTTOM: I pray you, commend me to Mistress Squash, your mother, and to Master Peascod, your father. Good Master Peaseblossom, I shall desire you of more acquaintance too. Your name, I beseech you, sir?

MUSTARDSEED: Mustardseed.

BOTTOM: Good Master Mustardseed, I know your patience well. That same cowardly, giant-like, Oxbeef hath devoured many a gentleman of your house. I promise you, your kindred hath made my eyes water ere now. I desire you of more acquaintance, good Master Mustardseed.

Bottom, when next we meet him, has grown familiar with his state, but he has not therefore lost his grip upon reality. He is willy-nilly King Consort in fairyland, but nevertheless an ass, a tender ass, very hairy about the face and in need of scratching. And being an ass, he appreciates the good things of an ass's life. Good hay, sweet hay, hath no fellow. He is also, through it all, Nick Bottom, the weaver, with a reasonable ear for music, expressed in a preference for the tongs and bones, and, in the matter of provender, a handful of dried peas. This is Bottom in all his glory. Let him blaze in extenso:

BOTTOM: Where's Peaseblossom?

PEASEBLOSSOM: Ready.

BOTTOM: Scratch my head, Peaseblossom. Where's Monsieur Cobweb?

COBWEB: Ready.

BOTTOM: Monsieur Cobweb, good monsieur, get you your weapons in your hand, and kill me a red-hipped humble-bee on the top of a thistle; and, good monsieur, bring me the honey-bag. Do not fret yourself too much in the action, monsieur; and, good monsieur, have a care the honey-bag break not—I would be loath to have you overflown with a honey-bag, signior. Where's Monsieur Mustardseed?

MUSTARDSEED: Ready.

BOTTOM: Give me your neaf, Monsieur Mustardseed. Pray you, leave your curtsy, good monsieur.

MUSTARDSEED: What's your will?

BOTTOM: Nothing, good monsieur, but to help Cavalery Cobweb to scratch. I must to the barber's, monsieur, for methinks I am marvellous hairy about the face—and I am such a tender ass, if my hair do but tickle me, I must scratch.

TITANIA: What, wilt thou hear some music, my sweet love?

BOTTOM: I have a reasonable good ear in music. Let's have the tongs and the bones.

TITANIA: Or, say, sweet love, what thou desir'st to eat.

BOTTOM: Truly, a peck of provender. I could munch your good dry oats. Methinks I have a great desire to a bottle of hay. Good hay, sweet hay, hath no fellow.

TITANIA: I have a venturous fairy, that shall seek
The squirrel's hoard, and fetch thee thence new nuts.

BOTTOM: I had rather have a handful or two of dried pease. But, I pray you . . . let none of your people stir me. I have an exposition of sleep come upon me.

TITANIA: Sleep thou, and I will wind thee in my arms.
Fairies, be gone, and be all ways away.

Bottom, playing before Theseus, is the victim of a bad tradition. Professional actors in presenting the lamentable comedy of Pyramus and Thisbe, conscientiously underline every point of the farce, embroider every absurdity and miss no opportunity for comic business. Burlesque is only tolerable in so far as it exposes intelligently the emptiness of a received convention, and it is effective only if played with solemnity. Its exponents must never seem to be aware of their absurdity:

PYRAMUS: Approach, ye Furies fell!
O Fates, come, come,
Cut thread and thrum,
Quail, crush, conclude and quell!

Shakespeare abundantly supplies the nonsense. Pyramus has nothing to do but speak with good accent and good discretion. There must never be any doubt of the sincerity of his *passion* (Theseus' own word). Does not Hippolyta herself declare: 'Beshrew my heart, but I pity the man'? Bottom's famous protest to the Duke is no mere impertinence but the forthright gesture of an artist anxious to be well understood. Theseus, with his interruption, is spoiling the game. He must be called to order and put right:

PYRAMUS: O wicked wall, through whom I see no bliss,
Cursed be thy stones for thus deceiving me!

THESEUS: The wall, methinks, being sensible, should curse again.

PYRAMUS: No, in truth, sir, he should not. 'Deceiving me' is Thisby's cue: she is to enter now, and I am to spy her through the wall. You shall see, it will fall pat as I told you. . . . Yonder she comes.

This is not self-centred insolence but the disinterested enthusiasm of an interpreter. Bottom's 'She is to enter now, and I am to spy her through the wall. You shall see, it will fall pat as I told you', recalls Hamlet's more famous interpolation: 'He poisons him i' the garden for's estate; the story is extant and writ in very choice Italian. You shall see anon how the murderer gets the love of Gonzago's wife'.

It may be argued, if satire be intended in this scene, the laugh is at the expense, not of Bottom enacting the woes of Pyramus, but of the lords and ladies who condescend to find it amusing. Theseus is kindly magnanimous:

> For never anything can be amiss,
> When simpleness and duty tender it.

> Our sport shall be to take what they mistake:
> And what poor duty cannot do, noble respect
> Takes it in might, not merit.

But condescension, however amiable, is still condescension, and some will prefer the royal good-fellowship of Bottom's 'Give me your neaf, Monsieur Mustardseed', or his friendly concern that Monsieur Cobweb shall not be overflown with a honey-bag. Incidentally, the Duke's commendation of 'tongue-tied simplicity' when he is about to encounter Bottom, who was never at a loss for the right word in a situation which would certainly have reduced his heroic Grace to a state of complete incoherence, is another of those accidental felicities of which (to repeat Hazlitt) it is too much to suppose that they are intentional but which very luckily fall out so. The Duke's comments on the play as delivered fall noticeably short of Bottom's observations on the play in preparation. These gentle auditors cannot hold a candle to Bottom for courtesy or apprehension and their treatment of Moonshine is downright impertinent. Demetrius interrupts him with the stale inevitable jest about the horns he should be wearing. Theseus pointlessly objects that the man in the moon should be inside and not outside the lantern and, when they have put the poor fellow out of his part, Demetrius with a clumsy deference caps his Grace's witticism—not only the man but his thornbush and his dog should also be in the lantern.

The laugh, then, is not all on one side where it is commonly assumed to lie. Who is Demetrius to deride the antics of Pyramus, a lover in moonshine? Was he not himself but a few hours since cutting a pretty poor figure in a wood near Athens, actor in the 'fond pageant' which Puck found so delectable. Lord! what fools these mortals be! But Demetrius must be excused where generations of English actors have so sadly mistaken Pyramus and his peers. Nothing is stranger or less creditable to the English theatre than the stage history of 'A Midsummer Night's Dream'. Shakespeare was barely cold in his grave when, to set on some quantity of barren spectators to laugh, Bottom and his company had sunk to the level of the grimacing officious clowns with whom we are only too familiar. The balance of the play had been so completely destroyed that it was alluded to in 1621 by a puritan censor of public morals as 'The Comedy of Pyramus and Thisbe' and in 1661 'The Merry Conceited Humours of Bottom the Weaver' were actually published as a separate piece, which was doubtless received by the wits of Whitehall in much the same spirit as by Demetrius in Athens. The seventeenth-century producers and critics simply did not know what to make of the comedy as a whole. Pepys in 1662 spoke for his generation: 'To the King's Theatre, where we saw Midsummer Night's Dream which I had never seen before, nor shall ever again, for it is the most insipid, ridiculous play that ever I saw in my life.' Pepys found nothing to the purpose except 'some good dancing and some handsome women, which was all my pleasure'. Thirty years later Betterton was producing an operatic adaptation which concluded with a chorus of Chinamen and a dance of six monkeys. The eighteenth-century stage was held for over forty years by an operatic enormity perpetrated by Richard Leveridge. Shakespeare's play became 'The Comick Masque of Pyramus and Thisbe' which, after spawning various successors, made way for the yet more complicated perversions of Garrick and Colman. Kemble at the beginning of the nineteenth century still regarded the play as a libretto for music and spectacle, much being made of a pageant showing the victories of

Theseus. This was the production that provoked a celebrated outburst from Hazlitt: 'All that is finest in the play, was lost in the representation. The spirit was evaporated, the genius was fled; but the spectacle was fine: it was that which saved the play. Oh, ye scene-shifters, ye scene-painters, ye machinists and dressmakers, ye manufacturers of moon and stars that give no light, ye musical composers, ye men in the orchestra, fiddlers and trumpeters and players on the double drum and loud bassoon, rejoice! This is your triumph; it is not ours: and ye full-grown, well-fed, substantial, real fairies . . . we shall remember you: we shall believe no more in the existence of your fantastic tribe.'[1]

The egregious Bunn was a fit person to bring this strange, eventful history to an ignominious conclusion with a compilation presented at Drury Lane in 1883 which outraged even the blunted sensibilities of the fashionable patrons of that august establishment. The tide was on the turn and in 1840 Charles Mathews and Madame Vestris brought back Shakespeare, or a piece of him, to the stage at Covent Garden.

But Bottom had suffered too severely from his many translations easily to recover his comic identity. Phelps produced the play at Sadler's Wells in 1853 and Bottom is reported to have been one of his best parts. The critics, however, give us no idea how he played it. They are more interested in recording that in this production gas was used for the first time in any theatre, that an effect of mist was conveyed by a seamless blue net expressly ordered from Glasgow and that the effect of movement was given by a diorama. One Shakespearean actor, the ever-to-be-lamented George Weir, has within living memory presented Bottom on the stage in a way that should have annihilated once for all the clodpole tradition of the professionally funny man which is the English theatre's legacy from three centuries of successful clowning. But Weir never found a successor even among the sons of Ben.

The stiff-necked generations which mistranslated Bottom saw so

[1] Hazlitt admired Liston in the part of Bottom, but tells us nothing about it, and it is most unlikely that this capable actor did more than present the character a little less clumsily than his predecessors.

little coherence or unity in the play that they used it for two hundred years as a quarry for fairy pantomime, burlesque, operatic miscellanies, masques and ballets. Bottom is so much the projection of Shakespeare's own imagination into this mimic world that, if we fail to identify ourselves with his immortal weaver, the comedy falls to pieces. No-one but he can sustain the triple illusion. He takes us along with him by virtue of the very quality which made it possible for Shakespeare himself to creep into the small soul of a fairy as easily as into the noble heart that cracked in the passing of Hamlet—a genius for accommodation with all things within the limits of his imaginable world. From first to last this is Bottom's dream and, if he come not, the play is marred.

But if he come in the habit with which Shakespeare invested him, the play creates for us a world in which we walk as securely as in a walled garden and, when the dream is ended, with Moonshine and Lion left to bury the dead, we may call back Hippolyta to speak the final word:

> But all the story of the night told over,
> And all their minds transfigured so together,
> More witnesseth than fancy's images,
> And grows to something of great constancy—
> But, howsoever, strange and admirable.

BEATRICE AND BENEDICK

Much Ado About Nothing

THERE is much ado in this comedy about innocent Hero slandered by her lover Claudio, led to believe by a villain, with no motive for his villainy, that she comes as no maid to her marriage. And all this, the author warns us in his title, is nothing; we are not to take seriously to heart any of that dreadful business at the altar steps but to regard the splenetic Don John as no more than a black bogey in a merry tale.

It is a Renaissance piece. A lady is wooed by proxy and married behind a veil. A diabolical lord contrives a plot which casts a shadow in sunlight. There are misunderstandings, obviously to be cleared up before the curtain falls. Beauty is shown in distress, virtue under a cloud and chivalry provoked. All this was extant and writ in choice Italian—the Italian of Matteo Bandello.

Bandello's story is just one of those agreeably silly tales from which in due course the lustier novelettes of yesterday were subsequently to be evolved. Claudio loves Hero. Don John, because he is superseded by Claudio in the good graces of his Prince, but more because he is temperamentally a bad man who hates to see other people happy, undertakes to prove her wanton. He succeeds in his design and Claudio denounces his bride in the church. Hero swoons and on the advice of a holy friar is reported dead. But the plot, as required by the laws of melodrama, is discovered by the funny man of the piece and Claudio finds his dead love surprisingly restored.

To recall these familiar incidents seems hardly necessary. But most people in thinking about 'Much Ado About Nothing' are apt to forget about Hero and Claudio. They remember it as a comedy about Beatrice and Benedick, as indeed it immediately became for the first audiences who saw it on the stage. Lord Treasurer Stanhope, paying John Heminge on May 20th, 1613, for a production of the play, actually refers to it as 'Benedicte and Betteris' and in a second

folio preserved at Windsor Castle you may see to this day, in the
handwriting of King Charles I, to whom it belonged, 'Benedick
and Beatrice' entered on the page as a second title.

This goes to show how very destructive two live characters can be,
let loose in a plot which depends for its verisimilitude on a different
kind of illusion. Benedick and Beatrice run away with 'Much Ado
About Nothing' as Mercutio would certainly have run away with
'Romeo and Juliet' if Shakespeare had not killed him off only just in
time. Whether Shakespeare meant this to happen is impossible to
say, but he certainly knew what he had done when, sitting back to
survey his work, he gave it a title which should plainly indicate that
his borrowed plot counted for nothing in his achievement.

This borrowed plot has been severely criticised. Let us first consider the objections.

It may be argued that the distresses of Hero accord painfully or not
at all with the gaiety of Beatrice and that the sable iniquity of Don
John is out of place in a comedy. But this is admittedly a composite
piece—Renaissance vertù was 'Q's' description, or as Walkley puts it
in 'Playhouse Pleasures', a polychromatic phantasmagoria or inn of
strange meetings. The whole thing is eclectic in the extreme, depend-
ing for its success on a skilful handling of contrasted styles, moods
and effects. It is the least natural of all the comedies. 'Love's Labour's
Lost' is straightforward Elizabethan horseplay compared with this
sophisticated amalgam of Italianate romance and light comedy. The
earlier play is on the surface more mannered; but if the artifice is
more apparent, that is only because Shakespeare in 1593 had not yet
learned to conceal it. In the later play every word, gesture and
sequence is contrived and measured to a hair. Of all Shakespeare's
plays it is the one in which his skill as a dramatist may best be studied
as distinguished from his genius as a poet and creator of character.
Even his own most personal contribution to the comedy, the affair
between Beatrice and Benedick, is a deliberate exercise in virtuosity
upon a given theme—in this case borrowed from himself. It is one of
his favourite themes, that of an attraction between lovers manifested
in a professed hostility. Shakespeare in 'Much Ado About Nothing'
relies almost entirely on his dramatic and literary craftsmanship, and

the success with which he conceals this fact from the critics who
receive this comedy as a spontaneous revelation of the careless, sunny
side of his nature shows that this man of the theatre, apart from being
Shakespeare, was as cunning a playmaker as ever deceived an audience
into accepting counters for true pay.

This disposes of the two-fold complaint (1) that Don John has no
right to be present in so light-hearted a piece and (2) that, being present,
he should have been provided with a more adequate motive. Don
John, in this formal pattern, is a dark square in a brilliant patchwork.
Shakespeare picks him up as he picks up his witty lady or his holy
friar—not as a human character to be presented for his own sake but
as a figure that looks well in the tapestry:

> I had rather be a canker in a hedge than a rose in his grace, and it
> better fits my blood to be disdained of all than to fashion a carriage
> to rob love from any: in this, though I cannot be said to be a flattering
> honest man, it must not be denied but I am a plain-dealing villain.

This fantastically wilful obliquity contrasts admirably with the no
less fantastical glitter of his environment—Saturn in conjunction
with Mercury.

Claudio, who so easily believes Hero to be false, who so brutally
exposes her to public ignominy and who for all this is rewarded
with good fortune and true love is more of a stumbling-block. But
it cannot be said that he is out of character. Shakespeare has carefully
fitted him for the ignoble part he is required to play. He is exhibited
from the first as ready to distrust himself, his friends and his lady. He
agrees that Don Pedro shall woo her by proxy but believes, at a hint
from Don John, that Don Pedro is playing false:

> 'Tis certain so—the prince woos for himself.
> Friendship is constant in all other things
> Save in the office and affairs of love:
> Therefore all hearts in love use their own tongues.
> Let every eye negotiate for itself,
> And trust no agent: for beauty is a witch
> Against whose charms faith melteth into blood:

> This is an accident of hourly proof,
> Which I mistrusted not. . . . Farewell, therefore, Hero.

Claudio's 'Farewell, therefore, Hero', prepares us in advance for the mistrustful levity with which he will listen to Don John affirming that Hero is 'disloyal' and that he shall 'see her chamber window entered even the night before her wedding-day'. 'May this be so?' is all he has to say when Don John has concluded his tale.

Claudio in church offends us less by his credulity than by his downright bad manners. Bad manners in a comedy of manners— that is an offence against the play itself. 'In the congregation where I should wed there will I shame her' is an idea that would never have occurred to a gentleman. And this is a comedy with gentility for a theme! There is no play of Shakespeare in which special deportment counts for so much; yet here is Claudio swearing to behave like an oaf. What is worse, Don Pedro accepts the project with alacrity. What was Shakespeare to do? There could never have been such a scene as Hero's wedding if everybody had behaved with ordinary decency. Claudio and Don Pedro are sacrificed to make a Sicilian holiday. Witness the scene in which these two gentlemen, after that business in the church and the reported death of Hero, comment on their encounter with Hero's uncle and father. *We had like to have had our two noses snapped off by two old men without teeth.* Witness their bantering of Benedick when he delivers his challenge. Witness, above all, the scene in which they acknowledge their error:

> CLAUDIO: Choose your revenge yourself,
> Impose me to what penance your invention
> Can lay upon my sin—yet sinned I not,
> But in mistaking.
> DON PEDRO: By my soul nor I,
> And yet to satisfy this good old man,
> I would bend under any heavy weight
> That he'll enjoin me to.

Was ever an apology more ungracious? Even in promising amends they protest that they were never to blame. Shakespeare, though, with a touch here and there, keeps these persons in character, using

H

them callously either to forward his plot or to throw into relief the comedy of Benedick and Beatrice.[1]

Attention has already been directed to the only circumstance which enables us to regard Claudio's behaviour as *theatrically* acceptable. Shakespeare artfully insists that Don John's plot will come to nothing. It is discovered by Dogberry *before* it is put into effect and publication is obviously postponed merely in order that the scene in the church may go forward. The mood in which we watch that scene is coloured by our knowledge that the constable is just round the corner waiting to put things right. The bad men are already under arrest and Leonato, if he had been less in a hurry to get to his daughter's wedding, would have got to the bottom of the mischief before it was sprung. But like Caesar ignoring Artemidorus and brushing aside the soothsayer on his way to the Capitol, Leonato goes blindly to his Ides; the scene in which he might have been warned *immediately* preceding the catastrophe. That, in itself, is an essentially comic situation and it is brought about by a device which has since become traditional in the comedy-melodrama of all ages. Villainy is undone by a simple soul. Dogberry is a trifle of Shakespeare's fancy, created for the double purpose of exposing a plot and confusing its delivery, but he is the ancestor of a comic figure which has held the stage from William Kempe to George Weir.

Shakespeare, it goes without saying, has done something else for Claudio, but no more than what he does for everybody in his comedies:

CLAUDIO: O my lord,
When you went onward on this ended action,
I looked upon her with a soldier's eye,
That liked, but had a rougher task in hand
Than to drive liking to the name of love:
But now I am returned, and that war-thoughts
Have left their places vacant: in their rooms
Come thronging soft and delicate desires,

[1] Shakespeare's handling of this scene between Claudio, Don Pedro and Benedick, one of the best in the play, if we focus our attention on Benedick, is discussed below, see pp. 131

> All prompting me how fair young Hero is,
> Saying I liked her ere I went to wars.
> DON PEDRO: Thou wilt be like a lover presently,
> And tire the hearer with a book of words.
> If thou dost love fair Hero, cherish it,
> And I will break with her, and with her father,
> And thou shalt have her: was't not to this end
> That thou began'st to twist so fine a story?

Claudio, like Bassanio, talks like an angel.

Having added this much more to all this much ado about nothing let us now turn to what is in effect the real business of the play. This is the comedy of Beatrice and Benedick in which Shakespeare used a fashion of the time to present a situation of abiding interest. The merry war between these self-professed misogamists is a courtship in disguise. It was a game which Shakespeare was always ready to play and, being a child of the Euphuists, he played it, if not *con amore,* at least without any great loss of integrity. We have seen what use he made of the wit-combat in 'Love's Labour's Lost'. Rosaline and Berowne prefigure Beatrice and Benedick, but in the later play Shakespeare is no longer concerned with its superficial absurdities, still less with exhibiting his own skill at the game. Wit which can so easily be tiresome is in Beatrice the natural overflow of a happy nature: 'But then there was a star danced, and under that was I born.' Her perpetual skirmishing is natural high spirits expressed, like everything else in the Elizabethan theatre, in a clatter of words— the Shakespearean equivalent of the knockabout contrived to amuse less loquacious generations or of the 'thwackings' which Boileau so severely deprecated in the comedies of Molière. Now high spirits fly at anything. It is hit or miss and, if we do not ourselves share in the rough and tumble for its own sake, we are more likely to find ourselves counting the misses than applauding the hits. Admittedly Beatrice is often pert rather than subtle:

BEATRICE: I wonder that you will still be talking, Signior Benedick— nobody marks you.

BENEDICK: What, my dear Lady Disdain! Are you yet living?

BEATRICE: Is it possible Disdain should die, while she hath such meet food to feed it as Signior Benedick? Courtesy itself must convert to disdain, if you come in her presence.

BEATRICE: I had rather hear my dog bark at a crow than a man swear he loves me.

BENEDICK: God keep your ladyship still in that mind, so some gentleman or other shall 'scape a predestinate scratched face.

BEATRICE: Scratching could not make it worse, an 'twere such a face as yours were.

and something of a hoyden:

DON PEDRO: You have put him down, lady, you have put him down.

BEATRICE: So I would not he should do me, my lord, lest I should prove the mother of fools.

But all this only the more firmly places her as a character—not the fine, brilliant, exquisite and witty lady of tradition but something of a bright young handful and irrepressible romp. Shakespeare continually insists on her merry heart which keeps on the windy side of care. She was 'born to speak all mirth and no matter'; and we have her father's word for it that 'she is never sad but when she sleeps and not even sad then, for . . . she hath often dreamed of unhappiness and waked herself with laughing'. That is why our pleasure in Beatrice survives the fashion of her wit and puts her among the immortal heroines of comedy. It is a pleasure in uninhibited youth and careless simplicity. There is no sophistication either of head or heart in Beatrice. Her emotions are as forthright as her social behaviour. When Don Pedro undertakes to get this chit a husband she 'would rather have one of his father's getting', and when Don Pedro offers to marry her himself she refuses with a 'No, my lord, unless I might have another for working days—your grace is too costly to wear every day'. The chit, as a chit, is irresistible. Whatever she may say, good or bad, awakes in us the pert and nimble spirit of mirth, turns melancholy forth to funerals.

Here are two young people professing an inveterate dislike. They never meet but they jar and each is equally exuberant in misogamy. They are brought artfully together by a conspiracy of matchmakers who convince Benedick and Beatrice in turn that each is dotingly in love with the other. But the plot, though it suggests with a playful indulgence, typically Shakespearean, that love is none the worse for a spice of human vanity, does no more than crown a foregone conclusion. For they are obviously interested in one another from the first—interested to the point of obsession. Their professions of dislike are inverted declarations of love. Don Pedro announces that he will 'undertake one of Hercules' labours, which is to bring Signior Benedick and the Lady Beatrice into a mountain of affection'. But Don Pedro exaggerates. It needed no great contrivance to bring these two together.

Shakespeare's inverted courtships—Berowne and Rosaline, Rosalind and Orlando, Katherine and Petruchio—in which love is expressed in a teasing conflict of wills and wits—are but one of the many delightful consequences of the fact that women were not admitted to the Elizabethan stage. Shakespeare wrote his love scenes for an audience which knew that his heroine was a man or boy dressed up to counterfeit a woman. The modern playwright, in handling a scene of sentiment or passion, has only to put a personable young man in close proximity with a desirable young woman and leave the rest to a few stammered words and disordered gestures. Shakespeare had no such easy way out. For a comedy courtship he must contrive plenty of amusing, familiar and lively conversation. For serious occasions only great poetry could serve his turn. The adolescent passion of Juliet and the immortal longings of Cleopatra had to be conveyed without any assistance from the infectious temperament or physical charms of a leading lady. The flesh and blood required by Shakespeare for his love scenes had to be supplied in prose and verse. To exhibit any form of sexual attraction, whether grave or gay, he must fire the imagination or tickle the fancy of his audience with words. What more exhilarating challenge could there be for a dramatic author whose genius throve on the solution of material difficulties? Confront Shakespeare with a technical problem and he accepts it as an opportunity.

'Much Ado About Nothing', as already suggested, is Shakespeare's nearest approach to the comedy of manners: the wit-combat between its predestinate lovers, besides being a favourite device of the author for establishing a lively familiarity between the parties, commits him to what is, in effect, the stock situation in a type of play which Congreve brought to perfection a century later. Beatrice and Benedick bickering their way into matrimony, are quite obviously assuming for our pleasure a social attitude which we know to be at variance with their true feelings and with the destiny which awaits them at the close.

In the pure comedy of manners as practised by Congreve sentiment or passion is conveyed by means of elegant understatement or downright contradiction:

MRS. MILLAMANT: I won't be called names after I'm married; positively I won't be called names.

MIRABEL: Names!

MRS. MILLAMANT: Ay, as wife, spouse, my dear, joy, jewel, love, sweetheart, and the rest of that nauseous cant in which men and their wives are so fulsomely familiar—I shall never bear that. Good Mirabel, don't let us be familiar or fond, nor kiss before folks, like my lady Fadler and Sir Francis, nor go to Hyde Park together the first Sunday in a new chariot, to provoke eyes and whispers, and then never to be seen there together again; as if we were proud of one another the first week, and ashamed of one another ever after. Let us never visit together nor go to a play together; but let us be very strange and well-bred: let us be as strange as if we had been married a great while; and as well-bred as if we were not married at all.

Millamant and Mirabel affect to have outgrown and overcome the promptings of nature.

The real point of the joke is that man is pretending to be civilised. This is the stock situation of the comedy of manners. The elaborate ritual of society is a mask through which the natural man is comically seen to look. The comedy of Millamant is that she is about to be married as a woman, and that she talks of her marriage merely like a person in society. In the comedy of manners men and women are seen holding reality away, or letting it appear only as an unruffled thing of attitudes. Life is here made up of exquisite demeanour. Its comedy grows from the incongruity of human passion with its cool, dispassionate and studied expression. It ripples forth in ironic contemplation of people born to passion high and low, posing in the social mirror. This is the real justification of the term 'artificial comedy' as applied to the plays of Congreve. We are born naked into nature. In the comedies of Congreve we are born again into civilisation and clothes. We are no longer men; we are wits and a peruke. We are no longer women; we are ladies of the tea-table. Life is absurdly mocked as a series of pretty attitudes and sayings. Hate is absurdly mirrored in agreeably bitter scandal. Perplexity and wonder are seen distorted in the mechanical turns of a swift and complicated plot. Always the fun lies in a sharp contrast between man civilised and the genial primitive creature peeping through. Artificial comedy is our holiday from the sublime and beautiful, from the coarse and the real. It is sublimation of the trivial, turning to fine art the accidents and trappings of life. It is essential to the comedy of manners that it should be well-gowned. It is the height of the comedy of manners that its protagonists should seriously encounter trifles.[1]

The comedies of Congreve and his contemporaries are slips from an Elizabethan forest intensively cultivated in a Whitehall garden. Millamant is a graft from:

BEATRICE: Lord! I could not endure a husband with a beard on his face —I had rather lie in the woollen!
LEONATO: You may light on a husband that hath no beard.
BEATRICE: What should I do with him: dress him in my apparel and make him my waiting-gentlewoman? He that hath a beard is more than a youth; and he that hath no beard is less than a man: and he that is more than a youth is not for me, and he that is less than a man I am not for him.

LEONATO: Well, niece, I hope to see you one day fitted with a husband.
BEATRICE: Not till God make men of some other metal than earth. Would it not grieve a woman to be over-mastered with a piece of valiant dust? To make an account of her life to a clod of wayward marl? No, uncle, I'll none: Adam's sons are my brethren, and truly I hold it a sin to match in my kindred.

MILLAMANT: There is not so impudent a thing in nature as the saucy

_____
[1] From the author's essay on Comedy, pp. 32–34.

look of an assured man, confident of success. The pedantic arrogance of a very husband has not so pragmatical an air. Ah! I'll never marry, unless I'm first made sure of my will and pleasure.

My dear liberty, shall I leave thee? My faithful solitude, my darling contemplation, must I bid you then adieu?

Compare Mirabel on Millamant with Benedick on Beatrice:

MIRABEL: Think of you? To think of a whirlwind, though 'twere in a whirlwind, were a cause of more steady contemplation; a very tranquillity of mind and mansion. A fellow that lives in a windmill has not a more whimsical dwelling than the heart of a man that is lodged in a woman. There is no point of the compass to which they cannot turn and by which they are not turned; and by one as well as another; for motion, not method, is their occupation.

BENEDICK: O, she misused me past the endurance of a block: an oak with but one green leaf on it would have answered her: my very visor began to assume life and scold with her. She told me, not thinking I had been myself, that I was the prince's jester, that I was duller than a great thaw—huddling jest upon jest with such impossible conveyance upon me, that I stood like a man at a mark, with a whole army shooting at me. She speaks poniards, and every word stabs: if her breath were as terrible as her terminations, there were no living near her, she would infect to the north star. I would not marry her, though she were endowed with all that Adam had left him before he transgressed. She would have made Hercules have turned spit, yea, and have cleft his club to make the fire, too. Come, talk not of her. You shall find her the infernal Ate in good apparel—I would to God some scholar would conjure her, for certainly, while she is here, a man may live as quiet in hell as in a sanctuary.

Congreve wrote the undiluted comedy of manners, distilling pure water from the living spring. His characters must sustain to the end their manifest pretences that they have no feeling deeper than an epigram may carry; no aspiration higher than a fine coat may express; no impulse stronger than a smile may cover; no joy more thrilling than a nod may contain; no sorrow deeper than a pretty oath may convey. Shakespeare's comedy, on the other hand, consists in elaborating these pretences in order that they may at the right moment be effectively exploded. Beatrice and Benedick, who begin by seeming least likely of any in Messina to betray a genuine emotion, must in the end uncover their hearts.

These wit-combats, whether in Shakespeare or Congreve, declare the sentiments which they affect to deny. As Witwoud puts it in 'The Way of the World': 'Raillery, madam, raillery; we have no animosity—we hit off a little wit now and then but no animosity. The falling out of wits is like the falling out of lovers—we agree in the main like treble and bass.' There is never any doubt that the raillery between Benedick and Beatrice is of this order. 'You must not, sir, mistake my niece,' says Leonato. 'There is a kind of merry war betwixt Signior Benedick and her. They never meet but there's a skirmish of wit between them.' These two are obviously treading a measure which will land them at the altar steps. Beatrice's first words are an inquiry after Benedick. He is the only man returning from the wars in whom she is interested. And Benedick is no sooner on the stage than he declares his admiration for Beatrice; for, when Claudio praises Hero as the sweetest lady that he ever looked on, Benedick retorts: 'I can see yet without spectacles, and I see no such matter: there's her cousin, an she were not possessed with a fury, exceeds her as much in beauty as the first of May doth the last of December.' 'Much Ado About Nothing' is no comedy of conversion in which disdain is by vanity transformed into affection. Our pleasure lies in waiting for the artifice of the wit-combat to be discarded as soon as nature asserts herself and the combatants are disarmed. This is the real comedy and we have it in full measure. For Benedick is ready to face all extremities for love, even to be laughed at for his pains, and when Beatrice needs a champion for Hero, this 'obstinate heretic in despite of beauty' comes to attention as her dutiful knight-at-arms.

Two devices are used to bring these declared antagonists to confession—the trick played on them by Don Pedro and his friends, whereby each is assured of the other's infatuation, and the impact upon them of Hero's calamity.

Observe how artfully Shakespeare contrives to get the maximum comic effect out of Benedick's apostasy. He loses no opportunity in the early scenes of asserting his misogyny:

DON PEDRO: I shall see thee, ere I die, look pale with love.

BENEDICK: With anger, with sickness, or with hunger, my lord—not with love: prove that ever I lose more blood with love than I will get again with drinking, pick out mine eyes with a ballad-maker's pen, and hang me up at the door of a brothel-house for the sign of blind Cupid.

DON PEDRO: Well, as time shall try: 'In time the savage bull doth bear the yoke.'

BENEDICK: The savage bull may—but if ever the sensible Benedick bear it, pluck off the bull's horns and set them in my forehead. And let me be vilely painted—and in such great letters as they write, 'Here is good horse to hire,' let them signify under my sign, 'Here you may see Benedick the married man.'

BENEDICK: I do much wonder, that one man seeing how much another man is a fool when he dedicates his behaviours to love, will, after he hath laughed at such shallow follies in others, become the argument of his own scorn by falling in love. And such a man is Claudio. I have known when there was no music with him but the drum and the fife, and now had he rather hear the tabor and the pipe: I have known when he would have walked ten mile afoot, to see a good armour, and now will he lie ten nights awake carving the fashion of a new doublet: he was wont to speak plain, and to the purpose (like an honest man and a soldier) and now is he turned orthography—his words are a very fantastical banquet, just so many strange dishes. May I be so converted, and see with these eyes? I cannot tell—I think not: I will not be sworn but love may transform me to an oyster, but I'll take my oath on it, till he have made an oyster of me, he shall never make me such a fool. One woman is fair, yet I am well: another is wise, yet I am well: another virtuous, yet I am well: but till all graces be in one woman, one woman shall not come in my grace. Rich she shall be, that's certain: wise, or I'll none: virtuous, or I'll never cheapen her: fair, or I'll never look on her: mild, or come not near me: noble, or not I for an angel: of good discourse, an excellent musician, and her hair shall be of what colour it please God.

All this, though it enhances the comedy of Benedick's transformation, at the same time prepares us for the event. The gentleman protests too much. Shakespeare, moreover, gives us some warning glimpses into the kind heart which hides behind all this exaggerated self-assurance. The man who said of Claudio in love, 'Alas, poor hurt fowl, now will he creep into sedges', is clearly a man of quick feeling.

Asked by this same Claudio for his opinion of Hero he demands:
'Do you question me as an honest man should do for my simple true
judgment or would you have me speak after my custom as being a professed tyrant to their sex?'—an obvious suggestion that we are to
distinguish between the attitude by which he is socially distinguished
and the simple sincerity which he owes to a friend. Then, again,
pondering his masked encounter with Beatrice, he exclaims: 'The
Prince's fool! Ha, it may be I go under that title because I am merry:
yea, but so I am apt to do myself wrong. I am not so reputed—it is
the base, the bitter disposition of Beatrice that puts the world into her
person, and so gives me out.' Benedick here shows himself uncom-
monly sensitive to opinion and, what is more to the point, to the
opinion of Beatrice. He is gay but would not therefore be thought
malicious; he makes a brave show of independence but would not
therefore be found conceited.

Don Pedro and his friends in the conduct of their plot play skilfully on their knowledge of the true man beneath the social mask,
attributing to him just those faults with which he most resents to be
charged. 'If she should make tender of her love,' says Don Pedro,
''tis very possible he'll scorn it—for the man, as you know, hath a
contemptible[1] spirit.' And again: 'I love Benedick well and I could
wish he would modestly examine himself to see how much he is unworthy so good a lady.'

The abrupt wholeheartedness with which Benedick at once embraces his fortune ('I will be horribly in love with her') is delightfully
absurd and at the same time increases our respect. This is no fool,
hoodwinked by an appeal to his vanity, but a man who seizes a
heaven-sent occasion to be himself. He easily capitulates because he
has never seriously wanted to hold out and he discloses in his
surrender the very modesty denied to him by his friends:

I must not seem proud. Happy are they that hear their detractions
and can put them to mending.

There is here no trace of self-infatuation: he is not in the least puffed
up on hearing that Beatrice is secretly in love with him:

[1] *i.e.* in the idiom of Shakespeare, a spirit easily contemptuous of others.

They say the lady is fair—'tis a truth, I can bear them witness: and virtuous—'tis so, I cannot reprove it: and wise, but for loving me—by my troth, it is no addition to her wit, nor no great argument of her folly.

The soliloquy in which Benedick forswears his assumed indifference and the subsequent scene in which Beatrice bids him come to dinner are a typical Shakespearean sequence. He is delightfully absurd ('Love me! Why, it must be requited. . . . If I do not take pity of her, I am a villain. If I do not love her, I am a Jew. I will go get her picture'). He is the victim of a conspiracy and the laugh is against him—as no-one knows better than himself:

I may chance have some odd quirks and remnants of wit broken on me, because I have railed so long against marriage: but doth not the appetite alter? A man loves the meat in his youth that he cannot endure in his age. Shall quips and sentences and these paper bullets of the brain awe a man from the career of his humour? No—the world must be peopled. When I said I would die a bachelor, I did not think I should live till I were married.

But his absurdity, far from exciting our derision, enlists our sympathy. This is no popinjay, but verily a good man and true. There is no better example in Shakespeare of the use of comedy to put us in full sympathy with its victims.

Beatrice, being a bird of more brilliant plumage than Benedick, suffers a yet more startling transformation:

HERO: Disdain and scorn ride sparkling in her eyes,
Misprizing what they look on, and her wit
Values itself so highly, that to her
All matter else seems weak: she cannot love,
Nor take no shape nor project of affection,
She is so self-endeared.

I never yet saw man,
How wise, how noble, young, how rarely featured,
But she would spell him backward: if fair-faced,
She would swear the gentleman should be her sister;
If black, why nature, drawing of an antic,

Made a foul blot: if tall, a lance ill-headed;
If low, an agate very vilely cut:
If speaking, why a vane blown with all winds;
If silent, why a block movèd with none.
So turns she every man the wrong side out,
And never gives to truth and virtue that
Which simpleness and merit purchaseth.

Thus must she hear herself painted by cousin Hero and the portrait fits the character she has so merrily assumed. But here again
Shakespeare has prepared us for the change. Beatrice, like Benedick,
protests too much—as we have heard. She is no genuine misogamist.
Witness her reaction to the betrothal of Hero with Claudio. Her
pleasure in that event looks through her merriment and there is even
a touch of envy, lightly expressed but not to be mistaken:

Speak, cousin, or, if you cannot, stop his mouth with a kiss, and let
not him speak neither. . . . Thus goes everyone to the world but I, and I
am sun-burnt. I may sit in a corner and cry 'heigh-ho for a husband'.

The expressed motive of her scorn for Benedick—and for husbands
because Benedick is already the only husband she will ever fancy—is
itself a clue to her veritable disposition. It is her grievance that Benedick is forever talking. He is Signior Mountanto. He affects, as she
does, high insolence towards the opposite sex:

I am loved of all ladies, only you excepted: and I would I could find
in my heart that I had not a hard heart, for truly I love none.

She is provoked by an assumed hostility which affronts her own un-
confessed inclination towards him and the more bitterly she rails the
more plainly she declares her affection. These two, indeed, are in the
same case. If Benedick is Signior Mountanto who will still be talking,
Beatrice is my Lady Disdain, a harpy who speaks poniards. They
attack in each other the insolent contentiousness that keeps them
apart and the collapse of their hostility is inevitable when each is presented to the other as horribly in love.

The capitulation of Beatrice is nicely contrasted with that of Benedick. Benedick, overhearing Don Pedro and his friends, is at first
suspicious:

I should think this a gull, but that the white-bearded fellow speaks it:
knavery cannot, sure, hide himself in such reverence.
This can be no trick. The conference was sadly borne.

In his soliloquy he is argumentative and looks at the situation all
round weighing the pros and cons. Above all, he cuts a comical
figure and knows it. It is far otherwise with Beatrice. Her soliloquy
springs straight from the heart. There is neither argument nor hesita-
tion. She has no thought to spare for the ridicule which her conversion may inspire, nor for its seeming inconsistency:

> What fire is in mine ears? Can this be true?
> Stand I condemned for pride and scorn so much?
> Contempt, farewell! and maiden pride, adieu!
> No glory lives behind the back of such.
> And, Benedick, love on, I will requite thee,
> Taming my wild heart to thy loving hand.

But Beatrice and Benedick, to be completely revealed, must not
be left as the mere victims of a comic mystification. Shakespeare
needed a more searching test of their quality and this is effected by
the emotional impact of Claudio's infamy. There were possibilities
of excellent fun with these two professed misogamists if Shakespeare
had brought them to a mutual confession of love as an immediate
result of the trick played on them in the orchard, but he preferred to
wait until they could meet upon an issue in which their feelings
were more deeply engaged. He gives us just a sample of the sport
he might have had with them when Beatrice calls Benedick to dinner,
and, in two symmetrical scenes, he shows us Benedick chaffed by his
friends and Beatrice teased by her cousin for their altered demeanour.
But he artfully postpones their confrontation until he can use the
plot against Hero to reveal them as 'human at the red-ripe o' the
heart'.

It is to be noted that even in the gay scenes preliminary to the
confrontation Shakespeare sustains the contrast to which he pointed
in the two orchard soliloquies. Benedick in his evasions is purely
comic. 'Gallants, I am not as I have been'—so much is too obvious
for denial. He has, so he affirms, the toothache and refuses to be

further drawn, but at the end of the scene he takes Leonato aside: 'I have studied eight or nine wise words to speak to you which these hobby-horses must not hear.' As a practical man, and Benedick is extremely practical, he has decided to approach the lady's guardian in good and proper form before paying his addresses to the lady herself. Benedick, in this scene, still alive to the fact that he is comic, is nevertheless not to be browbeaten. His appearance as a spruce young gentleman in love is an act of defiance and he bears himself in this scene with a manifest bravado. His friends may laugh themselves into fits but, true to his word, he will be 'horribly in love'.

Beatrice, in the corresponding scene with Margaret and Ursula, is more deeply stirred. There is none of Signior Benedick's bravado. She is 'exceeding ill' and sighs profoundly. She can hardly restrain herself from delivering the secret that fills her heart. Does she sigh for a hawk, a horse or a husband? 'For the letter that begins them all,' she answers, confession on the tip of her tongue. And there is not a flout in her—no single word of retort to the insinuations heaped upon her, merely such feeble protests as 'What pace is this that thy tongue keeps?'

The contrast conveyed in these scenes on the light comedy level is more deeply marked when these two brilliant creatures are suddenly confronted with a situation which calls into the open their rare qualities of heart and head. Watch their behaviour while the monstrous scene of Claudio's repudiation of Hero is in progress.

Benedick is the first to see that something is wrong. His quick mind takes alarm at Claudio's first obscure preliminaries. *How now! Interjections?* He would cover the situation with a laugh till Claudio's horrid bent is plain. Then it is he who makes the first comment: *This looks not like a nuptial.* The whole man, whom we now begin to know, is in those half-dozen words—a man whose quick mind and warm feeling find expression in ironical understatement. He is the first to show concern for Hero when Claudio has left the church: *How doth the lady?* The *lady,* mark you—she who has just been described by his Prince as a 'common stale'. He is the first to recover his wits. He is so attired in wonder that he knows not what to say, but his mind gets to work at once on the evidence and he asks, turning to Beatrice: 'Were you her bedfellow last night?' He is shaken and puzzled. Yet he goes straight to the point. Hero has been denounced by Claudio, Don Pedro and Don John:

> Two of them have the very bent of honour,
> And if their wisdoms be misled in this,
> The practice of it lives in John the bastard.

Finally, when the friar has made his proposal that Hero shall be given out for dead, Benedick stoutly declares himself:

> Signior Leonato, let the friar advise you,
> And though you know my inwardness and love
> Is very much unto the prince and Claudio,
> Yet, by my honour, I will deal in this
> As secretly and justly as your soul
> Should with your body.

Beatrice, meanwhile, has no reservations of any kind. She has no need of argument or evidence, but goes straight to the point. *O, on my soul, my cousin is belied!* She says nothing at all till Hero swoons and then it is the instinctive protest of one who would not herself have been so easily overcome: *Why, how now, cousin, wherefore sink you down?* She has no room for anything but love for Hero and hot indignation for the men who have so cruelly disgraced her. She is all air and fire; her other elements she gives to baser life.

The stage is thus set for the long-promised encounter in which Benedick and Beatrice, whose comedy was born in a merry hour, must prove that for all their gallant sophistication they can show a pair of hearts as sound and simple as any in Messina. We had never thought to see Beatrice moved to tears. But here she is, crying her eyes out, with Benedick standing awkwardly beside her and, all their tricks forgotten, love is confessed in the full tide of her wrath and *his* perplexity:

BENEDICK: Lady Beatrice, have you wept all this while?
BEATRICE: Yea, and I will weep a while longer.
BENEDICK: I will not desire that.
BEATRICE: You have no reason, I do it freely.
BENEDICK: Surely I do believe your fair cousin is wronged.

BEATRICE: Ah, how much might the man deserve of me that would right her!

BENEDICK: Is there any way to show such friendship?

BEATRICE: A very even way, but no such friend.

BENEDICK: May a man do it?

BEATRICE: It is a man's office, but not yours.

BENEDICK: I do love nothing in the world so well as you—is not that strange?

BEATRICE: As strange as the thing I know not. It were as possible for me to say I loved nothing so well as you—but believe me not—and yet I lie not—I confess nothing, nor I deny nothing—I am sorry for my cousin.

They must still spar a little, but they have ceased to find quarrel in a straw. The artificial wit-combat is now a genuine conflict of character. Benedick, though he believes Hero to be wronged, is still uncertain what he should do. Claudio, after all, is his friend. But Beatrice has no patience with half-measures, and a man is but half a man who will go with her only a part of the way:

BEATRICE: Will you not eat your word?

BENEDICK: With no sauce that can be devised to it—I protest I love thee.

BEATRICE: Why then, God forgive me——

BENEDICK: What offence, sweet Beatrice?

BEATRICE: You have stayed me in a happy hour, I was about to protest I loved you.

BENEDICK: And do it with all thy heart.

BEATRICE: I love you with so much of my heart, that none is left to protest.

BENEDICK: Come, bid me do anything for thee.

BEATRICE: Kill Claudio.

BENEDICK: Ha! not for the wide world.

BEATRICE: You kill me to deny it—farewell.

That, as everyone agrees, is the *clou* of the comedy. *Kill Claudio*—all we shall ever want to know of Beatrice is in those two words, and with what fire and eloquence she justifies her commandment:

BENEDICK: Is Claudio thine enemy?

BEATRICE: Is a' not approved in the height a villain, that hath slandered, scorned, dishonoured my kinswoman? O that I were a man! What, bear

her in hand until they come to take hands, and then with public accusa-
tion, uncovered slander, unmitigated rancour—O God that I were a man!
I would eat his heart in the market-place.

BENEDICK: Hear me, Beatrice——

BEATRICE: Talk with a man out at a window—a proper saying!

BENEDICK: Nay, but, Beatrice——

BEATRICE: Sweet Hero, she is wronged, she is slandered, she is undone.

BENEDICK: Beat——

BEATRICE: Princes and counties! Surely a princely testimony, a goodly
count, Count Comfect—a sweet gallant surely. O that I were a man for
his sake! or that I had any friend would be a man for my sake! But man-
hood is melted into curtsies, valour into compliment, and men are only
turned into tongue, and trim ones too: he is now as valiant as Hercules,
that only tells a lie and swears it. I cannot be a man with wishing, therefore I will die a woman with grieving.

Benedick no longer asks to be convinced. It is enough for him that
Beatrice shall declare herself to be sincere beyond all doubt.

BENEDICK: Think you in your soul the Count Claudio hath wronged
Hero?

BEATRICE: Yea, as sure as I have a thought or a soul.

BENEDICK: Enough, I am engaged.

The scene in which Benedick delivers his challenge to Claudio,
admirable in itself, is technically the most interesting in the play.
Why must Claudio descend from one base degree to another? In
Bandello's story he was a likeable young man. In Shakespeare's play
he is insupportable. We have glanced at his behaviour in church and
his subsequent callousness in the scene with Leonato and Antonio.
Even the soft and delicate desires, all prompting him how fair young
Hero is, are not confessed till he has ascertained that she will bring
her husband a fortune:

CLAUDIO: Hath Leonato any son, my lord?

DON PEDRO: No child but Hero; she's his only heir.

Shakespeare was notoriously casual in his handling of young
sprigs. Or perhaps in his careless charity he found them just so and
troubled too little about them to administer even poetic justice. But

Claudio is an extreme case and we can only assume that his author simply uses him to make a man of Benedick. Obviously he didn't greatly care what sort of man might marry Hero so long as he made it quite clear what sort of man should marry Beatrice.

In the challenge scene, Claudio, with Don Pedro to help him, odiously makes light of the situation for which he is responsible; but that is only because Benedick must show that he is dead serious. Don Pedro, speaking of his late encounter with Leonato and Antonio, flippantly remarks: 'I doubt we should have been too young for them.' That is a cue for Benedick to rebuke his Prince with a stern, becoming dignity: 'In a false quarrel there is no true valour.' Claudio, brushing aside the death of Hero and her father's distress, calls on Benedick to use his wit for their diversion so that Benedick may answer with crushing brevity: 'It is in my scabbard. Shall I draw it?' Claudio then seeks to entice him with one of those familiar wit-combats so that Benedick may rejoin: 'I pray you choose another subject.' Claudio must try to laugh Benedick out of his new-found honesty in order to show that Benedick is now fixed and constant as the northern star:

BENEDICK: You are a villain—I jest not—I will make it good how you dare, with what you dare, and when you dare: do me right, or I will protest your cowardice: you have killed a sweet lady, and her death shall fall heavy on you.

Don Pedro tries to save the situation with allusions to Beatrice, but this is no longer Benedick the Prince's fool and he doesn't so much as flinch when Claudio lets him know of the trick played on him in the orchard:

BENEDICK: You break jests as braggarts do their blades, which God be thanked hurt not. My lord, for your many courtesies I thank you. I must discontinue your company—your brother the bastard is fled from Messina: you have among you killed a sweet and innocent lady: for my Lord Lack-beard, there, he and I shall meet, and till then peace be with him.

After that, nothing is left but to prove that my lady Hero hath been falsely accused, and to bring in Benedick, the married man. He and Beatrice must still spar their way into matrimony, for 'thou and I are too wise to woo peaceably'. And before company they must still be talking:

BENEDICK: Come, I will have thee—but by this light I take thee for pity.
BEATRICE: I would not deny you—but by this good day I yield upon great persuasion, and partly to save your life, for I was told you were in a consumption.

But these two have shown themselves true lovers and none more devoutly than Benedick:

I will live in thy heart, die in thy lap and be buried in thy eyes: and moreover, I will go with thee to thy uncle's.

I'll tell thee what, prince: a college of wit-crackers cannot flout me out of my humour. Dost thou think I care for a satire or an epigram? no, if a man will be beaten with brains, a' shall wear nothing handsome about him. In brief, since I do purpose to marry, I will think nothing to any purpose that the world can say against it—and therefore never flout at me for what I have said against it: for man is a giddy thing, and this is my conclusion.

'Much Ado About Nothing' becomes in this happy conclusion the comedy of Benedick and Beatrice—a comedy that moves from sophistication to sympathy, showing how a true heart may be worn on an embroidered sleeve. It is the play of which Hazlitt wrote: 'Perhaps that middle point of comedy was never more nicely hit in which the ludicrous blends with the tender, and our follies, turning against themselves in support of our affections, retain nothing but their humanity.'

It is also the play on which Coleridge based a famous declaration concerning Shakespeare's plots: 'The interest in the plot is always on account of the characters, not vice versa, as in almost all other writers; the plot is a canvas and no more.'

Certainly there is no play of Shakespeare in which the relation of plot to character and character to plot can be more usefully studied. There could be no better instance of a plot used to exhibit the characters (Benedick and Beatrice) in which Shakespeare was specially interested. But the converse is equally true. No play affords a better instance of characters in which the author was not specially interested sacrificed to the main design. The characters of Claudio, Don Pedro and Don John are ruthlessly used—and some would say misused—to forward the plot of Beatrice and Benedick. The two procedures are not in fact either exclusive or contradictory. Shakespeare in all his plays has a story to tell—his own or, more usually, taken from someone else. He has to make that story credible on the stage and his characters are created for that purpose. They cannot choose but do what the story requires and to that extent they are determined by the plot. For Shakespeare's characters, imagined to begin with as the sort of people who will do what they have to do, come alive in the process. They may come so much alive that the author sometimes finds it difficult to control them or get them to fulfil their destiny. And almost invariably they are sufficiently alive to convince us that they are doing of their own will and pleasure what they were appointed to do by predestination. Our interest in the plot, as Coleridge says, is on account of the characters, but it does not follow that the characters are doing just as they please. Shakespeare, creating for the stage, reflects a paradox already created in the world by Providence —free will must be squared with necessity.

Coleridge's distinction, right as far as it goes, is thus in the last analysis unreal. The give and take between character and plot in Shakespeare is as fluid as between character and circumstance in real life. Shakespeare, writing for the stage, had to present men in action. For a dramatist it is what men *do* that matters—in other words the plot is capital. But we are interested in what men do because they are men and therefore apparently free to do as they please. Coleridge quotes as a crowning proof of Shakespeare's 'interest in the plot being always on account of the characters' an instance which really cuts both ways. He describes Dogberry and his comrades as being forced into the service of the plot *when any other less ingeniously absurd watchmen and night constables would have answered the necessities of the action.* Dogberry, in other words, is to be regarded as an instance of Shakespeare's interest in character prompting him to create a group of persons imagined for their own sake and endowed with qualities not essential to the dramatic business in hand. But this is not so. The characters of Dogberry and his comrades, however much they may seem to exist by their own right and to abound freely in their own sense, are exactly determined by the part they are called upon to play in the comedy. It is not true that any other less ingeniously absurd watchmen and night constables would have answered the necessities of the action. Dogberry has to be sharp enough to discover there is a conspiracy against Hero *before* it is executed, so that the audience may know in advance that all will come right in the end. But he must also be stupid enough to prevent his discovery from taking effect till the conspiracy has served its turn. The character of Dogberry—his prolixity, his reverence for the protocol, the facility with which he meanders from the high road of detection into the by-paths of mystification, the slow mind that wastes itself upon irrelevant details but keeps obstinately moving in the right direction, the self-centred zeal that attaches as much importance to being written down an ass as to establishing that his prisoners have verified unjust things and, to conclude, are lying knaves—corresponds exactly with the necessities of the action. Dogberry, in fact, is a supreme example of the way in which Shakespeare, creating his characters to fit a pre-determined plot, brings them so abundantly to life that they seem to exist entirely for their own sake and to be following their own devices. Dogberry had to be just that sort of man for the things he had to do. Yet here is Coleridge regarding him as created by Shakespeare for the mere fun of the thing! Shakespeare's craft as a playwright successfully conceals the fact that Dogberry was expressly designed to forward—or perhaps we should say to retard—the action of the play. Shakespeare's genius in creating character nevertheless deceived Coleridge into selecting Dogberry as a supreme example of a character who, so far as the necessities of the plot are concerned, need never have been created at all.

No better text could be found in which to study the interplay of Shakespeare's dramatic art of character and situation than this most brilliant but least profound of his major achievements. To Benedick and Beatrice, once he has decided that this is to be *their* comedy, everything is sacrificed within the limits of dramatic coherence and plausibility. Don John's conspiracy is used to warm their hearts and enliven their understanding. Claudio, sacrificed in advance to the necessities of this merely secondary plot, is put without mercy through his ignoble paces so that Beatrice may show something of the generous stuff of which my Lady Disdain is made and so that Benedick may reveal that Signior Mountanto, in despite of fortune and fashion, is prepared to defy his Prince and to challenge his friend. The distresses of Hero, though necessary to the comedy, must not, however, be allowed to cast too deep a shadow. We must therefore know in advance that Don John's machinations will come to nothing. For this purpose Dogberry is haled from an Elizabethan township to play the part of a *deus ex machina* in a Sicilian city—and this he does to such perfection that he seems to be there for no better reason than that his author has taken a sudden fancy to the man and gives him free leave to come and go as he pleases.

And somehow the whole thing hangs together; an 'inn of strange meetings' where everything, or nearly everything, is accepted as we go along, a 'polychromatic phantasmagoria' in which the colours blend into one composite picture. 'Much Ado About Nothing' is not one of the great comedies. But it is one of Shakespeare's greatest triumphs as a dramatic craftsman, showing what he can do when his genius is not half engaged and he falls back on his technical skill as a playwright.

Shakespeare, on completing this comedy, might have addressed the friend of his heart, had there been such a man, in the words addressed by Hamlet to Horatio:

> They are coming to the play; I must be idle:
> Get you a place.

PRINTED IN GREAT BRITAIN
BY ROBERT MACLEHOSE AND CO. LTD.
THE UNIVERSITY PRESS, GLASGOW